Persuasive Writing of All Kinds: Using Words to Make a Change

Lucy Calkins and Elizabeth Dunford

Photography by Peter Cunningham

HEINEMANN ◆ PORTSMOUTH, NH

This book is dedicated to my grandparents, for their love, guidance, and patience, even through my most persuasive moments. —Elizabeth

This book is dedicated to my father, Evan Calkins, who has helped me understand that I come from a long legacy of men and women who have used writing to try to make the world a better place. —Lucy

Heinemann
361 Hanover Street
Portsmouth, NH 03801–3912
www.heinemann.com

Offices and agents throughout the world

© 2013 by Lucy Calkins and Elizabeth Dunford

Cataloging-in-Publication data is on file with the Library of Congress.

ISBN-13: 978-0-325-04723-2

Production: Elizabeth Valway, David Stirling, and Abigail Heim
Cover and interior designs: Jenny Jensen Greenleaf
Series includes photographs by Peter Cunningham, Nadine Baldasare, and Elizabeth Dunford
Composition: Publishers' Design and Production Services, Inc.
Manufacturing: Steve Bernier

Printed in the United States of America on acid-free paper
20 19 18 17 16 VP 10 9 8 7 6

Acknowledgments

THIS BOOK HELPED US REALIZE that it is indeed true that writing is not just desk work; it is life work. Although our organization, the Teachers College Reading and Writing Project, has worked for six years now to develop, pilot, learn from, and deepen units of study in persuasive writing, the call to choose the one and best plan was challenging for us. Our ideas were still, we felt, very much in formation. To write this book, then, we had a lot of teaching, planning, brainstorming, researching, learning, and talking to do, even before one word was fastened to the page.

That learning process was nurtured by a think tank on argument writing that is sponsored by the Council of Chief School Officers and brings the Teachers College Reading and Writing Project into a collaboration with the CBal section of ETS, and especially allows us access to the thinking of Paul Deane, who has been an influential researcher of argument writing for years. We are grateful for the CBal team.

Meanwhile, this is also a unit on kindergartners as writers, readers, and learners. To think about best practice ways to bring these robust young thinkers into the world of debate, petitions, persuasive letters, and the rest, we've spent a long time learning from colleagues at the Teachers College Reading and Writing Project. We are especially grateful to Amanda Hartman, associate director of the Project, who has a leadership role in primary staff development, and to Sarah Picard Taylor, whose earlier book on this topic blazed trails for our book. Three staff developers have played especially important roles in our thinking about this topic and in keeping us both feeling supported: Shanna Schwartz, Lauren Kolbeck, and Lindsay Wilkes.

Of course, the book relies not just on knowledge about kindergartners and about argument writing, but also on knowledge about the teaching of writing. The methods of teaching that inform every page of this book are the result of three decades of research into best practices in teaching writing. Many people think of methods of teaching writing as one monolithic thing, but because we are part of a think tank that has invested decades in developing more and more robust methods of teaching writing, we approach the work of planning a unit with so many thought tools in hand. We come at this knowing that there are ten different methods one can use in a minilesson—inquiry, guided practice, demonstration, peer conferring, proficient partner, and on and on the list goes. We know, too, about methods for small-group work and about methods for using charts to support independence. All of that knowledge has informed this book.

An extraordinary team at Heinemann invested themselves heart and soul into this book. Three people lead that team: Kate Montgomery, who has been at the helm of all the Units of Study series, Teva Blair, who has joined Kate as a senior editor of this gigantic project, and Abby Heim, who has been the production mastermind and a wise voice of counsel and direction for the entire project. Felicia O'Brien, once a teacher at a TCRWP school and now an editor, gave this book her loving care, and we thank her as well.

But more than anything, this book benefits from the brilliance of children and their teachers. We are especially thankful to the teachers and children at PS 682 in Brooklyn, whose hard work is celebrated across the pages of this book. Your enthusiasm for learning and the belief that words can make a world of difference has been an inspiration to us, and we know it will be to others.

The class described in this unit is a composite class, with children and partnerships of children gleaned from classrooms in very different contexts, then put together here. We wrote the units this way to bring you both a wide array of wonderful, quirky, various children and also to illustrate for you the predictable (and unpredictable) situations and responses this unit has created in classrooms across the nation and world.

—Lucy and Liz

Contents

Acknowledgments • iii

Welcome to the Unit • vi

BEND I   Exploring Opinion Writing: Making Our School a Better Place

1. Words Are Like Magic Wands: They Can Make Things Happen • 2

In this session, you'll teach students that just as magicians use magic wands to make things happen, writers use words.

2. Convincing People: Providing Reasons and Consequences • 11

In this session, you'll teach students that the more reasons they can provide, the more convincing their writing will be.

3. Don't Stop There! Generating More Writing for More Causes • 20

In this session, you'll teach students that opinion writers cast a wide net when writing, writing in a variety of genres and to a variety of audiences.

4. Writers Reread and Fix Up Their Writing • 28

In this session, you'll teach students that writers do not wait for others to tell them how to revise their writing. They reread what they have written and think, "What can I do to make my writing better?"

5. Spelling Strategies Give Writers Word Power • 36

In this session, you'll teach students that writers call upon many strategies to figure out how to write words that are hard to spell.

6. Hear Ye! Hear Ye! Writing to Spread the Word (a Mini-Celebration) • 44

In this session, you'll teach students that opinion writers get their words out into the world to enable change.

BEND II   Sending Our Words Out Into the World: Writing Letters to Make a Change

7. Writing Letters that Reach Readers • 54

In this session, you'll teach students that writers write letters as if they are talking to their reader.

8. Studying a Mentor Text (a Guided Inquiry) • 65

In this session, you'll teach students that writers read and study the work of other writers and then try to incorporate what they have learned into their own writing.

9. Knowing Just What to Say: Angling Letters to Different Audiences • 74

In this session, you'll teach students that when writers are working to make a difference, they write letters to many different people, angling those letters to the different audiences.

10. How Can We Make It Better? Imagining Solutions • 82

In this session, you'll teach students that persuasive writers include possible ideas for how to fix the problem they are writing about.

11. Wait! What's That Say? Fixing Up Letters before Mailing Them • 92

In this session, you could teach students that before writers send their letters out into the world, they reread their writing to make sure it is clear and easy to read.

Bend III   Persuasive Writing Projects

12. Draw on a Repertoire of Strategies to Write about a World Problem • 96

In this session, you'll teach students that when writers want to tackle new, ambitious projects, they draw on all they know—in this case, all they know about writing persuasively.

13. Sound Like an Expert! Teaching Information to Persuade Your Audience • 105

In this session, you'll teach students that persuasive writers make their writing convincing by including facts that teach their readers important information about their topic.

14. More on Adding Detailed Information to Persuasive Writing • 112

In this session, you could teach students that writers read about their topic so they can include more detailed information in their writing. Or, you might teach students that writers reread their writing to see where more precise details can go.

15. Writing How-To Books to Make a Change • 116

In this session, you'll teach students that writers can write how-to books to give their readers detailed instructions about how to solve a problem.

16. Editing for Punctuation: Partner Work • 123

In this session, you could teach students that writers reread their writing to be sure they have included the right punctuation that will tell their readers how to read their piece.

17. Speaking Up and Taking a Stand: Planning and Rehearsing Speeches • 127

In this session, you'll teach students that writers make a plan for the ideas they want to share when giving a persuasive speech.

18. Fixing and Fancying Up for Publication Using the Super Checklist • 136

In this session, you'll teach students that writers revise and edit their writing before publication using writing tools, in this case a checklist.

19. The Earth Day Fair: An Author's Celebration • 143

In this session, you could teach students that when writers write to make a change, they share their writing with others, calling their audience or readers to action by answering their questions and asking them to add their name to a petition or a sign-up sheet.

Welcome to the Unit

WHEN TEACHING CHILDREN TO WRITE, you teach them not only to spell, to link sentences, and to use examples. You also teach them a way of living in the world. You give them an identity, and an image of what's possible.

As a teacher of kindergarten children, you invite youngsters to live the life of being an actively engaged reader and writer. You show children not only how to write, but also why to write. You show them that writing is for real purposes. Writing involves making letters to be mailed, songs to be sung, chants to be performed, speeches to be made, petitions to be circulated, signs to be displayed. Jerry Harste once said, "Your job, as teachers, is to create a richly literate world in the classroom and then to help your children role play their way into being the readers and writers you want them to be." That is exactly what you do in this unit.

In this unit, you teach kindergartners that they can write to make their classroom, their school, and their world into a better place. You help them know that they are not just writing "pieces" for folders. They are writing particular kinds of texts for specific audiences. Because they are writing for real audiences, it is especially important for them to think about what their readers will need to know and to write with audience awareness.

Of course, your children will be writing not just for real-world reasons. They'll also be writing so they develop their skills to meet and exceed the CCSS for kindergarten and also, frankly, for first-grade opinion writing. The Common Core prioritizes opinion/argument writing, even including a special section titled "The Special Place of Argument in the Standards" (CCSS, Appendix A, p. 24). By the time your students graduate from high school, the Common Core expects them to "write arguments to support claims in an analysis of substantive topics or texts, using valid reasoning and relevant and sufficient evidence" (W 1). It may seem strange to be thinking about your

students' entering college when they have just started their school careers, but the Common Core expects that education is focused on that end result, so the steps to achieving it start now. Thus, this unit lays the foundation for some of the work the Common Core considers essential to students' academic and professional success.

In kindergarten, children are merely expected to compose opinion pieces in which they "tell a reader the topic or the name of the book they are writing about, and state an opinion or preference about the topic or book" (CCSS W K.1). Students are expected to do this work through using a "combination of drawing, dictating, and writing." This unit expects that kindergartners can do work that is far beyond this, and it therefore teaches them to exceed the expectations of the Common Core.

OVERVIEW OF THE UNIT

The unit is designed so that children do lots and lots of persuasive writing. They begin by writing signs, songs, petitions, and letters about problems they see in their classroom and their school, and then they address problems they identify in the larger world of their neighborhood. As they progress toward addressing concerns that are not right underfoot, that tackle slightly more distant topics and address more distant audiences, they meanwhile also learn more about persuasive writing and about writing in general. With your help, children apply what they learn not only to the newest piece they are about to write but also to their growing folder, full of completed pieces.

The first portion of the unit—the first bend in the road—is called "Exploring Opinion Writing: Making Our School a Better Place." From the very start of this unit, you'll ask children to look at the world around them in new ways—seeing not just what is, but what could be. You'll teach children to reflect on the troubles they see around the classroom and school and think, "What could make things better?" and to then do all kinds of writing to help make a change. You'll offer students a menu of possibilities for the writing they'll do during this first part of the unit. Perhaps they'll design signs or posters to catch people's attention quickly, telling them about a problem and what they wish would change. Maybe instead, some writers will make lists, naming all the ways the playground could be better, or make up some new rules for a sibling to follow. A child might decide to make a petition, asking every kid in the class to sign his name, agreeing to help get things done. This is not a time to assign students to write in a particular genre or to address particular issues; instead, you offer a menu and urge them to consider even more ways they could write to make a change: a book, a song, a card, a letter. The choices are endless.

Regardless of the genre, your kindergartners will be learning to make words (and pictures) to express what they want. You'll teach strategies for convincing an audience. Five-year-olds do a lot of persuasive speaking all the time, so part of your job will be to help children see that when they argue for a new pet, they're using language in ways that they can bring into this new kind of writing. At the close of this first bend, you'll help students celebrate their work by posting signs in the hallways, reading pieces to schoolmates in other classrooms, reciting songs over the school loudspeaker, and using the bullhorn at recess to rally friends to sign a petition. As children send their words out into the school they'll learn that by writing they can convince others to make the world better.

In the second part of this unit, you'll channel students toward writing lots of persuasive letters. This time, you'll guide them to use their words to make things better in the neighborhood, branching out from problems they see in the classroom or at school. To start this bend, you'll remind writers that to make a change in the world, it helps to ask, "Who could help me fix this problem?" Then, you'll teach children that they can write letters to persuade people to join the cause. You'll help children write lots of these letters, to lots of people, addressing lots of problems. Although it would be easy for you to fan the flames of concern around a particular issue and to channel all this letter-writing fervor toward that shared cause, this portion of the unit is intended to support lots of independent initiatives. Your goal is to teach kindergartners that when they want to create a change, it is important to convince people to agree with them, and letter writing is one important way to do that. As part of the unit, you'll teach children that adding facts and information to a letter

helps to make it more persuasive. You'll also teach that tucked within their persuasive letters, they may embed how-to texts. At the end of this bend, you'll again give students an opportunity to celebrate their work, perhaps with a class trip to the post office or to the nearest mailbox.

In the third, and final, bend of this unit, you'll rally kids to join you in a whole-class pursuit, possibly around a more global cause such as protecting the planet. You'll again invite children to write in a variety of genres, asking them to work on individual projects that convince others to "be green!" Students might use poster boards to display this array of new writing, designing a collage of signs, songs, petitions, letters, lists, how-to books, and so on. You'll remind writers to recall everything they have learned about persuasive writing this month and apply these strategies when writing new pieces, too, and you'll also teach them ways to lift the level of their persuasive writing.

To prepare for the final publication, you'll provide opportunities for partners to work together to rehearse their writing out loud. Together, partners will plan how their presentations might go, using body language, facial expressions, and gestures to show the big feelings they have about their topics. You'll help your young politicians captivate their own audience, using a long pointer to share the parts of their projects, reading parts of their writing, and speaking freely about their ideas and opinions to convince others to help in this larger cause. You might create some fanfare around this writing celebration; have students stand on soapboxes around the gymnasium or schoolyard or up on stage in the school auditorium to share their projects with others. In any case, you'll celebrate the persuasive writing your students have worked on across the unit, reminding them of the larger purpose—sharing opinions and convincing others to make a change.

ASSESSMENT

Before you begin this unit of study, you will want to collect some data to support your planning and to allow you to track the results of your teaching. Presumably you will have given children an on-demand writing task in opinion writing at the start of the year. You will in any case want to give another on-demand assessment just prior to embarking on this unit. This will help you assess your students' grasp of this new genre, as well as pinpoint the most current needs of your writers. We recommend you prompt this writing by saying the following to your children the day before the assessment. (We know it will go right over their heads, but say it so that the conditions in which kindergartners write will be comparable to the conditions in which older students write—and at some point, they need to bring in alternate sources.)

> "Think of a topic or issue that you know and care about, an issue about which you have strong feelings. Tomorrow, you will have forty-five minutes to write an opinion or argument text in which you will write your opinion or claim and tell reasons why you feel that way. When you do this, draw on everything you know about essays, persuasive letters, and reviews. If you want to find and use information from a book or another outside source, you may bring that with you tomorrow. Please keep in mind that you'll have forty-five minutes to complete this, so you will need to plan, draft, revise, and edit in one sitting."

Then the next day, repeat the relevant parts of this, and give the children forty-five minutes to plan and write. Don't help them! You'll again wince at ways this prompt do not seem appropriate for kindergarten children, and we agree with that. But because we plan to take the work that your children do and merge it with work first- and second-graders do, and for example, because second-graders' work will be merged with third- and fourth-graders work, it ends up being important to keep the prompt the same for children at different grade levels. The truth is that your kindergarten children will hear the parts of this that they understand, and the rest will fall by the wayside. Although the prompt may seem unintelligible, we've actually seen amazing results from kindergartners.

You'll also remind your writers to make sure they:

- Name their opinion
- Use details to show why they have that opinion
- Make an ending for their opinion piece

If you do adapt this prompt—for example, leaving out mention of essay writing or bringing in related information—we encourage you to plan this in conjunction with your grade team to ensure that you gather consistent data that you can compare across the grade.

Once the students have done this, you'll want to score their work. You can use the exemplar pieces from the Opinion Writing Learning Progression and the corresponding Rubrics for Opinion Writing—Kindergarten. As always, know that if your kindergarten writers reach a level K on the rubric, they will be meeting end-of-year expectations. To do this, they'll need to tell, draw, and write about an opinion and to say more about that opinion using words like *because* and including details in pictures and words. The unit is designed to help students develop skills that are regarded as first-grade skills in the CCSS and on our checklists, making your students highly proficient from the git-go. Be sure to assess the extent to which students have met those skills.

After your students publish their final pieces of persuasive writing, you will once again ask them to compose an on-demand piece of writing. This on-demand will serve as a summative assessment, measuring growth across the unit. Are students writing with greater detail and incorporating strategies to persuade an audience, such as including supporting reasons? Is the piece more structured, starting with a clear statement of opinion? Are students now meeting or exceeding grade-level expectations?

GETTING READY

In preparation for the launch of this unit, you'll want to provision your writing center with baskets of paper choices, offering a variety of templates for persuasive writing. For example, you may include a basket of letter-writing paper, along with envelopes and postage labels, blank poster paper for signs, poetry paper for songs or chants, and perhaps even petition paper with a space for signatures. Samples of these paper choices can be found on the CD-ROM. Whichever paper choices you choose to include, you'll want to differentiate for the needs of your writers, offering options that include a space for drawing to support planning and elaboration and stapled booklets with additional lines for writing to encourage increased volume. You may also choose to immerse your students in the voice and structure of the persuasive writing they'll soon engage in through read-aloud and shared writing of letters, petitions, signs, or even songs. You may even choose to read books that contain persuasive writing such as *Click, Clack, Moo: Cows that Type* by Doreen Cronin or *Corduroy Writes a Letter* by Alison Inches. Engaging your class in this work can help set the stage for the work they'll do as writers across this unit.

Words Are Like Magic Wands

They Can Make Things Happen

IN THIS SESSION, you'll teach students that just as magicians use magic wands to make things happen, writers use words.

GETTING READY

✔ Students in established writing partnerships, although you may elect to alter some of these

✔ A variety of paper choices including poster paper for signs, letter-writing paper, stationery for cards, poetry paper for songs, and narrative paper (picture box and lines) for petitions or opinion books 📀

✔ "Writers Write to Make the World Better!" chart (see Connection and Teaching)

✔ Sample of student-written petition (see Share) 📀

COMMON CORE STATE STANDARDS: W.K.1, RI.K.7, RI.K.8, RI.K.10, SL.K.1, SL.K.2, SL.K.3, SL.K.6, L.K.1, L.K.2

TODAY YOU WILL LAUNCH A UNIT in persuasive writing. You'll teach your youngsters to reflect on the troubles they see and to think, "What could make this better?" and then to work toward making those possibilities come true. As part of this unit, you'll teach kindergartners that writing is a way to act on the world, and persuasive writing is a way to organize collective action. You won't talk about "collective action" in so many words, but you will help children persuade others to join a cause.

You might question whether it is appropriate for five-year-olds to organize their own versions of marches on the White House. Do you really want to open the Pandora's box of encouraging children to use writing to make their world a better place? Might you end up deluged with petitions for more play time and fewer vegetables at lunch?

The Common Core is not ambivalent: a big part of educating young people to be college- and career-ready involves helping them use writing as a tool for expressing and challenging opinions. (It also emphasizes couching one's arguments in well-reasoned logic and supporting them with valid evidence.) The standards are also clear that critical literacy is for children, not just for secondary school students.

And it is very much within developmental reach for kindergartners to see troubles, imagine possibilities, and rally others to join a cause. In fact, children often master the fine art of persuasion long before they start school! This unit taps into their instincts to pursue the greater good, channeling those instincts toward using writing to make classrooms, schools, neighborhoods, and the world better. Across this initial bend, you'll demonstrate that writers can choose topics by thinking of problems they encounter every day, by living with open eyes, seeing what is and imagining what could be.

You, as well as the children, will want to transfer all you have learned from earlier units to this unit. While your children should remember that sketching and writing-in-the-air are ways to plan remind yourself that early in a unit, it is important to accept approximations with hope and good cheer, not beating yourself or your kids up when their writing looks like the work of a novice. After all, this is a new beginning.

Words Are Like Magic Wands

They Can Make Things Happen

CONNECTION

Tell children that you see problems in the world that you wish you could fix, citing a few, and ask whether they've ever seen problems as well. Use this to drumroll to work on persuasive writing.

Once children convened on the rug, I slouched in my chair, rested my head in my hands and let out an exasperated sigh. Then, with a furrowed brow, I said, "Writers, sometimes when I am in our classroom, I see problems around me that I wish I could change. When I look around, I sometimes see markers and crayons on the floor and think to myself, 'I wish we could work together and take care of our materials better.' When I sit in our classroom library, I think, 'This library would be even better if there were more books to read. I wish we could fill those baskets more.' And when I meet the class in the recess yard and I see kids pushing, I wish that the kids would be better friends and play more nicely at recess.

"Have you ever had a problem that you wished you could fix?" A flurry of thumbs shot up as I scanned the rug before continuing.

"Well, you don't have to just *wish* these problems go away. You can *write* them away. I'm telling you this because people don't just write stories and how-to books. People also write ideas and opinions. You can use writing to say exactly what you think. Just like a magician uses a wand to make things happen, writers use words. You can write to help solve problems and to help make our classroom and our school even better."

❖ **Name the teaching point.**

"Today I want to teach you that if you are going to write to make the world a better place, first you need to ask, 'Where is there a problem?' After thinking of a problem, you think of ways to solve it. Then you write to make things better."

Play this up! Be a ham. And of course you'll want to replace this list of words with your own.

This is favorite line for me: you don't just wish and hope problems go away. You can write them away! Qualities of good writing matter in mini-lessons. When you write your own minilessons, you'll find that you hit upon some sentences that have parallel structure, and then when you sit in front of your class, trying to recruit and hold their attention, you will feel the power of those rhetorical structures.

> Writers Write to Make the World Better!
>
> 1. See a problem.
>
> 2. Think.
>
> 3. Write.

TEACHING

Demonstrate thinking of a problem in the school or neighborhood, thinking of a way to fix it, and then asking, "Could I write something to make things better?"

"I've been thinking that maybe, just maybe, you all would be up for spending our next unit doing lots and lots of writing that doesn't just go in folders or on bulletin boards, but that actually makes the world a better place. Would you be willing to try doing that?" The children eagerly nodded their heads in agreement.

"First, you need to think about the classroom or the school, and think, 'What problems do I see? What could be better?'" I let the room grow silent as I silently generated my own ideas. Then, as if surprised by my own great idea, I said, "Oh! I've noticed a problem that has been happening in the hallway. Sometimes, I see people running!"

I paused. Mission (half) accomplished. I had thought of a problem. I visibly relaxed, as if the job was done. Then the children watched me catch myself, realizing with a start that I still needed to take the next step. After that, I asked myself, "What could be a way to fix this?" I again paused, this time musing to myself, "I think the hallways at school would be better if people *walked*."

Then I referred to the chart listing steps to take and mused to myself, "Could I write something to someone that might get people to be more careful in the hallway? Hmm. I'm thinking that *maybe* I could write a book about this problem and read it aloud to the kids. Then maybe the kids would slow down."

Debrief by describing what you have done in a way that children can transfer to their own writing.

"Writers, did you see how I, (1) thought about the problems I see and then, (2) thought about how to fix them, and then, (3) I thought about how I could use writing to make things better? Now I am going to write a book about the problem and read it aloud to others."

You could easily think of a problem and a way to solve it in the blink of an eye. But just as we teach upper elementary kids to "stretch out the heart of the story," you are stretching out the heart of this minilesson. You are making this process which can be instantaneous for you into a much more elaborate one, so that kids can see what it entails.

ACTIVE ENGAGEMENT

Channel writers to share problems they see and to imagine ways they could write to address the problems.

"Now it's your turn. Right now, will you stop and think about a problem you see? Something *you* think could be better?" I voiced over as the children thought quietly. "Maybe that problem is in our classroom, or in our school, or outside at recess." After a minute, I said, "Tap your chin when you've got an idea, so I know you're ready to share what you're thinking." Once I saw that students across the rug had ideas, I prompted, "Turn and share your opinions with your partner. When you talk, will you go a step farther and talk about, (2) how you could fix things and, (3) if you could write something to someone, in a way that might help."

The children started talking and I listened in.

Jack turned to his partner and quickly blurted out, "My problem is the markers and the glue sticks. They're all dried out and then we can't use them!" I coached Kevin, his partner, to ask how writing could help. Jack thought for a moment. "I think I can make signs all over the room, that tell the kids, 'Don't dry them out anymore.'"

Meanwhile, nearby, Melody said, "My problem is sometimes the kids talk when the teacher is talking and they don't listen and then I can't hear."

I nudged her partner to ask, "How can you fix that?" but Melody was stumped.

Coach into children's work, using voiceovers to help them go the next step and think about the kind of writing they could do, and the audience they need to address, to solve the problem.

"Class," I said, speaking over the hubbub. "Sometimes it helps to think, 'Could I write a letter to someone to help? A book for people to read? Could I write an announcement to read over the PA system? A sign? A song? A list of rules? A list of reminders?'"

As I finished making that point, Melody gestured that she could make a list of reminders for the class. "I can tell the other kids some of the rules for good listening when the teacher is talking!" she said.

LINK

Repeat what you have heard partners share in ways that spotlight the broad range of ideas for writing that the class has generated.

"Writers, I am hearing so many different opinions about the things you can change! Kevin wants people 'to play nice' at recess, so he is going to write a list of recess rules. Jaden thinks we need more blue paint, so he is going to write a letter to our principal asking for that."

As you run through the steps, reference the chart. Do this repeatedly. Sometimes when you do this, signal children to join in, reading the words of the chart as in a shared reading.

If none of the children seem to grasp what you want, and you don't hear any of them coming up with ideas like this one, don't hesitate to put words into their mouths. You know the issues the class finds troublesome. Perhaps lunch is way too late and they are always hungry. If so, say to a child who seems stuck, "Is the late time for lunch one of your problems?" Once the child has nodded a vigorous yes, you can then tell the whole class about the work this one child has done, using his work (which is really your work) as a model.

The active engagement section of a minilesson is meant as a time for guided practice, so expect that usually you'll call out a few voiceovers or children talk in partnerships. Sometimes you'll find the kids need even more support, in which case you might share five or six children's decisions as a way of modeling the sorts of thinking you hope all students are now doing. If you found children were floundering and shared examples so as to support them, give them additional time to generate ideas after you shared those examples.

Remind children of the challenge you've posed. Engineer things so those needing support stay in the meeting area while others get started.

"So remember, today and every day you can think, 'What problems do I see in our classroom or school? What ideas do I have for how things could be better?' And the really exciting thing is that you can use writing to help make things better.

"You might write signs or petitions, lists or books, rules or letters. But the important thing is that you write something that you hope will help to fix a problem. You will need to think about a problem in the school and do something very, very grown-up—write in a way that will get someone else, and maybe lots of people, to help you solve that problem and make things better.

"Right now, will you give me a thumbs up if you have figured out what problem is that you are going to fix?" I wasn't surprised that most of the children had that firmly in hand. "Now, a harder question. Will you give me a thumbs up if you have decided what you are writing, and to whom?"

When half the class signaled that they had ideas, I said, "Tell your partner exactly what you plan to write today." After children talked for a bit, I said, "If you know what you are doing, rush to get started. If you aren't sure what to do, stay in the meeting area."

You may feel tempted to keep kids on a shorter leash, asking them all to write one kind of persuasive text. For example, you might be tempted to ask them to each write a letter to the principal. Resist that temptation. Trust us that it's a great thing to issue a wide open invitation, and to see what children do in response. After all, what's the worst thing that could happen?

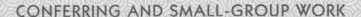

Conferences that Launch a New Unit

ALWAYS AT THE START OF A NEW UNIT, you will want to confer in ways that rally youngsters to become invested in the new work. It can help to think about times in your life when people have responded to your work in ways that lifted the level of your investment. What is it that others have done that made you tackle the endeavor with great ambitiousness and zeal? For me, I've always found that I rise to the occasion when others show that they believe in me. I recall Donald Murray, perhaps the greatest writing teacher ever, who once described his conferring by saying, "I see more in my students than they see in themselves. I find they are authorities on subjects they think ordinary." Murray was my teacher, and I will never forget the swelling confidence and determination I felt when he leaned forward in his chair, eyes fixed on me, listening raptly to all that I told him about whatever the topic was that I'd selected. His listening pulled words out of me, making me have more and more to say.

Now, decades later, I know that I have a long way to go before I listen to children as Murray listened to me. It's so easy to take in what they say in a distracted way, nodding pleasantly while your eyes dart this way and that. To launch the unit well, try to make a deliberate decision to listen with full-hearted attention. As you do this, remember that you are listening not just to the writing, but to the child's identification of a problem in the world, to the suggested solution, and to the child's idea for how writing might help. This is a three-step process that you are asking youngsters to undertake (although actually you can merge the second and third steps so this is thinking about a problem and then thinking about ways that writing can help with that problem). Either way, this is a bit of a challenge. Then, on top of that, you are asking children to essentially identify a genre, a topic of writing, and an audience for writing! That's a tall order.

This means, of course, that you need to be ready to welcome approximation. When Jack, in a turn-and-talk time during the minilesson, announced that he planned to solve the problem of the dried-up markers and glue sticks by making a sign, my instinct was to nudge Jack to imagine a more ambitious writing project. I refrained from doing that. The truth is that even though a sign may not be an especially ambitious writing

MID-WORKSHOP TEACHING   Writers Live with Open Eyes, Seeing Problems and Possibilities Everywhere

I stood in the middle of the workshop and spoke loudly enough to grab everyone's attention. "Writers, some of you did very quick writing, and you are almost finishing the letter, the sign, the book, that you wrote, so I want to help you think of other topics you can write about during this *Writing to Change the World* unit. Here is a tip. If you are ever stuck on what to write about, it helps to live with open eyes, looking at things around you in the world and thinking, 'How could this be better?'

"Let's practice! Pretend you are stuck on what to write." I acted out the part of a frustrated, blocked writer, rolling my eyes, lifting my hands in an exasperated pose, and encouraged the children to do this too. "Wait! We don't just need to sit here, feeling stuck! We can *do* something! Let's try the strategy of living with open eyes, seeing what is right before us." I looked around to see what was before me, and the first thing I saw was the coat closet.

"Let's take the coat closet—and think, 'How could the coat closet be better?'"

I left a pool of silence. "Oh my goodness, I can see so many ideas bursting out of you. Don't say them. Hold them in. Now think, what could you write? A speech? A sign? A list of rules? A letter? A song? How can you take your ideas for improving our coat closet and actually make something better happen?

"But writers, if you are stuck," I returned to my dramatization of a stuck writer, "I am not saying write about the coat closet. No way! The answer is to live with open eyes and to see what is right in front of you, and to think, 'How could this be better?' Like, look over here. Look at the hamster's cage or at the math center or at the library. What ideas do *you* have for how one of those could be a better place? Right now, tell your partner four ideas that are coming to you as you look with open eyes." The children talked. "Writers, if you finished your first piece of writing, you can always write about one of those ideas you just got from living with open eyes. Get to work!"

project, it is not a small accomplishment for a five-year-old to identify a problem in his life and to generate the idea of making a sign to address that problem. Good for him.

Of course, the other thing that will be important today is that you are ready to scaffold your children's work. If a youngster can't imagine what he or she could make to solve a problem, be ready to show the child how you go about thinking about this. You could say something like, "I usually say to myself, 'Is there someone I could write to who might help?' Then after that, I think, 'What should I write to that person?'" Then again, instead of showing the child a replicable process that he or she could use often, it can also be helpful simply to provide training wheels for the child, suggesting a kind of writing, an audience, so the child can get started all the sooner with your help. You might even go so far as to muse aloud over a way to start the writing, then dictate that lead to the child. That way, you give the child an experience that he or she would not otherwise have had, and set the child up to be able to work with more independence next time.

Learning from Other Writers

Remind children that writers learn from other writers, and invite children to inquire into what another writer has done that they could transfer to their own writing.

After the children gathered in the meeting area, I began. "You already know that writers find work they admire and think, 'What did this writer do that I could try, too?' We can learn not only from published authors, but also from writers who are regular people, just like us. For example, I think we can learn something by looking at this writing that a kid who lives near me did. Maura wrote *a petition* to fix the problem she has been noticing in our neighborhood. A petition is a kind of writing that opinion writers can make when they want to say, 'All these people think you should . . .' Usually the people sign their names to show they agree.

"Let's read Maura's work, and let's each think, 'What did she do in her petition that I could try in my writing?'" I displayed Maura's booklet (see Figure 1–1), so students could see her work as I read across the pages.

FIG. 1–1   You can pretend Maura lives in your neighborhood and share this petition (see CD-ROM) or better yet, share work written by one of your children.

"What did Maura do to help people understand her problem and convince them to help fix it?" I gave children a minute to think and then said, "Turn and tell your partner things Maura did that you could try in your writing and your pictures."

Paul told his partner, Shane, "She put talking bubbles in the picture." Shane stared up at the text, unsure of where she'd done that, until Paul pointed to where Maura had written, "Woof." He said, "See—the dog is talking!"

I moved on to another partnership, which again focused on the dog's bark, but this time they talked about the use of capital ("big") letters. Philip explained, "It makes the word *loud*." I reconvened the group and asked a partnership to share its observations. I jotted these down, knowing that later I would want to make an enlarged copy of the writing, with descriptors in the margins of the text. I summed up the class's work by reminding children that when they wanted help, they could live with open eyes, and they could learn from other writers.

FIG. 1–2   Maura's marked-up petition

Convincing People
Providing Reasons and Consequences

YOU HAVE ALREADY BEGUN TEACHING your students to look around with eyes that see not only what *is*, but also what could be, and now you will want to help them learn to write in ways that convince others. As you tackle this challenging work, you'll meanwhile want to notice whether a few writers are still struggling to generate topics, as those children will need small-group instruction.

The work of helping writers write in ways that convince readers will last this entire unit and will, of course, be work that children continue to study throughout their school careers. Your instruction in opinion writing will build on your children's oral language abilities. Face it. Some children will enter this unit with tremendous skills at influencing people. These will be the children who already use their rhetorical prowess to get an extra recess, a second read-aloud, a class pet. In this unit, your goal will be to help *all* children learn to use language, evidence, and logic to persuade. The opinion writing expectations in the Common Core are not high for kindergartners. Your children are merely expected to introduce a topic and state an opinion or a preference about that topic. But there is nothing holding you back from teaching your youngsters to do work that far exceeds these standards, and we recommend this. Within a few years, the expectations of the Common Core rise steeply, and your students will benefit from entering fourth grade with lots of experience in this genre under their belt.

You will want to write your own demonstration text. You can, of course, write a marvelous text that is light years beyond anything your youngsters could ever produce, but actually it is helpful if you produce a text that is just beyond your children's zone of proximal development. You'll probably want to write an early draft that is filled with some of the problems children will produce in their writing. You'll find that when your draft mirrors the work that the bulk of your class is doing, then you can use your text to teach children how to spot and address common issues.

Spotting problems in your children's writing won't be a hard thing to do! When you look over the work that your children produce, chances are good that it will seem as if they're slipping backward now that they have shifted to opinion writing. You'll probably

IN THIS SESSION, you'll teach students that the more reasons they can provide, the more convincing their writing will be.

GETTING READY

✔ Teacher demonstration piece to model the work of adding reasons (see Teaching) This writing becomes a chart paper book eventually, with a line or two of text under the picture. See Figure 4–1 for the text you eventually write.

✔ Student writing from previous session (see Active Engagement)

✔ Student writing that models techniques for writing persuasively (see Share)

COMMON CORE STATE STANDARDS: W.K.1, W.K.5, W.1.1, RL.K.2, RI.K.8, SL.K.1, SL.K.2, SL.K.3, L.K.1, L.K.2, L.K.6

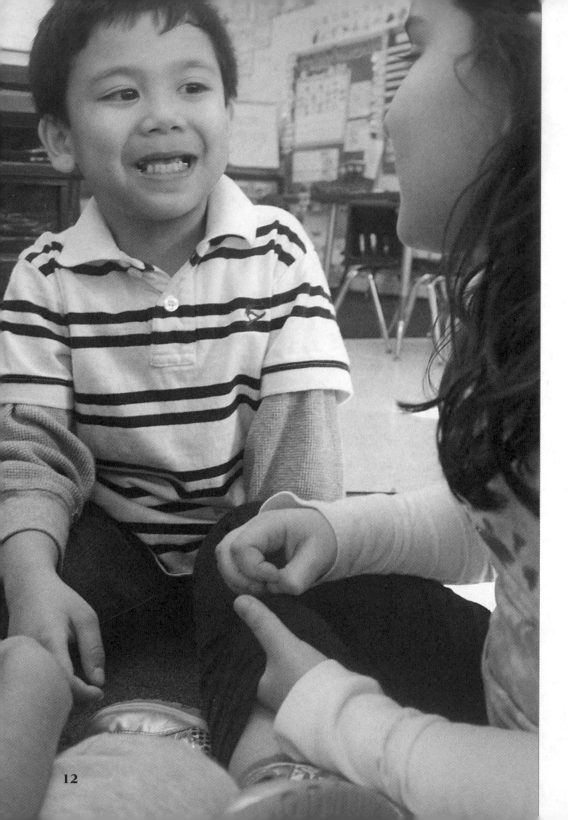

find yourself longing for the well-developed stories and how-to books that your children used to produce. Don't despair! This is a new genre, and you shouldn't expect that children will approach it with well-developed skills. Remember that when you bring children to any new genre, it is crucial for you to welcome approximation.

"In this unit, your goal is to help all children learn to use language, evidence, and logic to persuade."

In this session, you'll teach children that to persuade people to do something, it is important to show them the reasons the action is important, and to share the possible consequences of doing nothing. Additionally, you'll demonstrate how opinion writers can do this with pictures and words—adding details to drawings, speech bubbles, and sentences.

Convincing People
Providing Reasons and Consequences

CONNECTION

◆ COACHING

Tell children about someone who was influential—perhaps the Pied Piper—and suggest that their goal is to write in ways that rally people to follow.

"Writers, have you ever heard the fairy tale story of a boy who was called the Pied Piper? He went through the town playing a flute, and all these cats followed him. A cat would be sleeping on a little girl's bed, hear the Pied Piper, and jump up. 'Me-ow, me-ow,' the cat would say, and it would run out to follow the Pied Piper. Soon there was a whole parade of cats, following this Pied Piper.

"Writers, I'm telling you this because if you want to use writing to make the world better, then you need to be a little like the Pied Piper. *But* you need *people*, not *cats*, to follow you.

"For example, if you come up with the greatest idea in the world for keeping our coat closet clean, and you even stayed in one recess to get the new system started, but if then no one else followed your idea, what would happen to the coat closet?" The children all agreed it would look as bad as ever in no time.

❧ **Name the teaching point.**

"So, writers, today I want to teach you that you can be like the Pied Piper, getting people to follow your idea, and you can do this using words, not a flute. One way that sometimes works to get people to follow your idea is to give people lots and lots of reasons why they should follow your idea. The more reasons you can give them, the more convincing you will be!"

TEACHING

Tell children that you are not convinced something you wrote the preceding day is convincing (make it not be!) and mull over how to make it more persuasive.

"Yesterday we talked about how kids running in the hallway has become a big problem in our school. Last night I took some time and started to draft a book about this. But now, I'm not sure that it's very convincing. I don't know if people

When using a metaphor, don't elaborate excessively. The only thing children need to know about the Pied Piper is that he was persuasive. He got people—well, cats—to follow him, parading through town. Adding a lot of other details will only complicate the comparison you want to make.

Note that the examples of ways to change the world that we suggest early in the book are all situated within the classroom and the school. In later bends in this unit, examples will affect the larger community.

I think the hallways could be
better because sometimes
people run. Don't run!

FIG. 2–1 The demonstration text before you add more reasons.

are actually going to follow the suggestions I made. Can you reread my draft and think if there are ways you can help me make it more convincing?"

> I think the hallways could be better, because sometimes people run. Don't run!

"I'm wondering how we could make it so when kids hear this book read aloud, they think, 'Yup, that's right. We really better not run so much.' Hmm. I'm wondering how we could make this more persuasive."

Show children that writing is more apt to persuade people to take an action if it cites multiple reasons why an idea should be followed.

I waited to see if a child would repeat the teaching point, pointing out it helps to say lots of reasons why it is important to fix the problem. No one pitched in that idea, so I continued. "Oh! Now I remember. It sometimes helps to tell people *lots of reasons* why they should fix the problem.

"Hmm, let's think about more reasons why people should fix this problem, more reasons why it's a bad idea to run in the hallways." I paused to ponder while children eagerly raised hands to offer suggestions. "Okay, I have an idea! Here's a reason: It is dangerous to run in the hall. Someone might fall, or crash into another person. Kids could get very hurt! We should add that." I began sketching and writing this, although I did not finish doing this before talking again to the class.

Recap your process in ways that emphasize the transferable aspect of this strategy.

"After I draw this, I'll write some sentences about it as well. Did you see what we just did? We realized our writing was not that convincing and decided we needed to persuade people by adding more reasons to support the opinion. We reread our opinion and thought hard about a reason we could add. In this case, we gave a reason that supports the opinion that kids should stop running in the hallways."

ACTIVE ENGAGEMENT

Channel children to tell each other how they would make the writing they did the previous day more convincing by adding in more reasons.

"Now it's your turn to try! Take out the writing you did yesterday. Think about the problem you were hoping to solve, and think, 'What is *another* reason why people should help me solve this problem?'"

I gave the class a moment to rehearse and then said, "Turn and talk." As children talked, I added, "Make sure to tell your partner what you can add—the exact words that you might write."

You'll notice that we're not suggesting you start right away emphasizing the importance of incorporating reasons into your argument. Instead, we're suggesting that you first note that your writing is not convincing and only then come to the realization that you haven't included reasons and need to do so. This is actually a pattern you will see in most teaching components of a minilesson. When teaching kids how to generate topics for writing, the first thing you are apt to do is to suggest you are stuck, unable to think of what to write. Then, after encountering this problem, you show writers a strategy they can use to get themselves out of the problem. You are doing the same thing here. Strategies are a deliberate, conscious sequence of actions one takes to achieve a purpose. Eventually they become internalized and are done unconsciously, quickly, underground, at which point they cease being strategies.

Notice that you are always watching the time. The important thing to show is the process of generating reasons, not the process of drawing.

I listened to Serena tell her partner, "I think that all the kids should stop taking the Legos home." Her partner, Zaara, shrugged but said nothing. I prompted her to ask Serena, "*Why* should kids stop taking the Legos home? Why is that so important?" Once those girls were discussing what Choice Time would be like if there were no Legos left in the classroom, I moved on to another partnership.

LINK

Remind children that their writing will be more convincing if they include many reasons.

"So from now on, remember that one of your biggest jobs as an opinion writer is to find problems in the world, to think of ways to fix things, and then to use writing to convince people to help fix the problem. You can be more convincing if you give your readers *lots* of reasons."

Channel writers to revise the writing they wrote previously to make it more convincing and to then write more.

"Today I bet you are going to want to go back to the writing you already did (and some of you wrote two pieces of writing yesterday) and to see if you can make those pieces of writing more convincing, so that your writing helps you act like the Pied Piper. After working to make yesterday's writing more convincing, I know you will get going on another piece of writing. Soon you are going to have a whole folder full of writing!"

As you listen in to partnership talk, when you find yourself wanting to coach a writer, try suggesting the partner do this coaching instead of you. Whisper a suggestion to the partner.

Notice that this gathers up, consolidates, all you have taught this far in the unit.

It's great when the ending of a minilesson can link back to the connection, as this reference to Pied Piper does. Notice the cues you are giving to help youngsters know that they are expected to produce a lot of writing.

Conferring to Ensure that Your Minilesson Is Reaching Students at Varying Ability Levels

YOUR CHILDREN PROBABLY MADE SIGNS, cards, and brief letters during yesterday's workshop. They're probably done with that work. Today's minilesson, then, asks them to reread their finished work and to return to that work to revise it. Your first job today, then, will be to nudge writers to get started rereading and revising. You'll want to create some upbeat energy about the grand project of revising writing so that your children don't grow up thinking that revision is anything but a compliment to good writing. If you want to fuel excitement for revision, bring out special supplies. "Revisers can use lots of colorful paper for adding on," you can say, and produce slips of colored paper, tape, and staplers. You will find that children are excited about the carpentry of revision, even if they are less enthralled with the prospect of adding reasons to support their opinions.

Once children are rereading to revise, you may want to remind them of other lenses they can bring to their rereading. For example, during the previous units, writers learned that they can reread and ask, on every page, "Did I do at least one special thing on this page?" What wonderful transference it would be to bring that strategy into this new unit. The good news is that adding something special to each page is an open invitation, and writers will find it easy. They're probably more able to do that than to add reasons to support their opinions.

If it is hard for your children to generate a couple of reasons to support their opinions, encourage them to use their fingers to count off reasons. Voice over and coach them as they name reasons across their fingers with language stems such as, "One reason is . . ." "Another reason is . . ." Then prompt them to add those reasons to their writing.

For your more proficient writers, you can help them know that they can not only mention the reasons why their readers should take action, but they can also provide their readers with possible consequences of inaction. "Kids should stop running in the hall *or else* someone could fall and hurt themselves." By helping a few of your stronger writers do that, you'll provide examples that the others can follow.

MID-WORKSHOP TEACHING
Providing Consequences of Inaction to Persuade

"Writers, can I interrupt? Eyes up here," I said and waited for their attention. "How many of you have not only revised the writing you did yesterday but also already started a piece of writing today?" I scanned the room and noticed lots of hands up. "Great! Earlier you learned that one way to be like a Pied Piper, getting people to follow your ideas, is to provide people with *lots* of reasons why they should follow your idea. That is just *one* way to convince people. Another way—one that might be even more important—is this. You can tell them that if they don't do something, the problem might get *worse and worse*!

"So if I want you to walk quietly in the hallway and not to run, it not only helps for me to give *lots* of reasons. It also helps for me to tell you what could happen if you *don't* follow my idea. 'Kids should stop running in the hallway, *or else* someone might fall down.' I could make it worse, too. 'They might hit their head on the wall and get bumps and bruises. Or kids could crash into each other!' And if Serena wants kids to stop taking Legos home, she can give an *or else*. Stop taking Legos home, *or else* we won't have enough to play with at Choice Time. We'll only get to play with Play-Doh.

"Now it's your turn to try! Think about the writing you are working on right now. Think about the problem you were hoping to solve, and think, 'What if people don't help? What could get worse and worse?' Give me a signal to show you have ideas to share."

I gave the class a moment of time to rehearse and then asked them to turn and talk to the kids at their tables. As children talked, I added, "Make sure to talk about what you can add—the exact words—that will get people worried about how things could get worse and worse if they don't help."

For example, as I approached Serena, I noticed that she was rereading a letter she'd started the day before. All on her own, I watched her add another sentence to a taped-on revision strip. As I sat down beside her, she looked up at me and proudly held up a scroll-sized piece of paper, made from combining several sheets. "What are you working on today?" I asked. "This is my letter to all the kids who take the Legos. They take them to their house and they don't bring them back," she explained. She proceeded to read her letter aloud, pointing with the end of her pencil as she reread each word (see Figure 2–2).

> Dear kids who takes Legos. We're missing. We need them out of your house if you forgot it. Teachers get sad if you don't bring it. Teachers are sad. Bring it back.

"Serena, can I give you a compliment? You are doing something that opinion writers do to get people to help them. At the very beginning, you explain the problem." I pointed to the words in her text that did that. Then I added, "Do you notice what you do next?" I helped Serena see that next, she tells her readers what they should do to fix the problem. She pointed to the part of the text that accomplished this while I smiled to myself at the thought that at the age of five, she was already engaging in the sort of close reading and text citation work that the authors of the Common Core extol.

She added, "Yeah, and if the kids don't bring the Legos back, then we can't play at Choice Time and then there's only Play-doh and the other blocks, and not Legos," she rattled on.

As Serena spoke, I knew this conference would lead me to support the one thing I teach more than anything else when working with young writers. I'd lured Serena to say more, and now I was going to get her to add that added elaboration into her draft. Whether children are writing narratives or informational writing or arguments, it will happen time and again that they write in skeletal fashion and that conferences lead them to generate more content. To me, whenever I employ the conferring move that I knew lay ahead of me, I try to not only get the writer to add more, but to also *teach* the writer *how* to add more. I try to remember the admonition that I gave teachers decades ago in *The Art of Teaching Writing*: "If the piece of writing gets better and the writer learns nothing that can help another day with another piece, the conference was a waste. Teach the writer, not the writing" (1994).

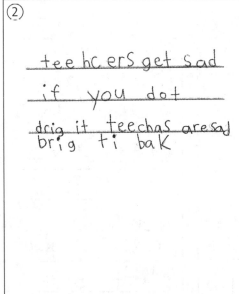
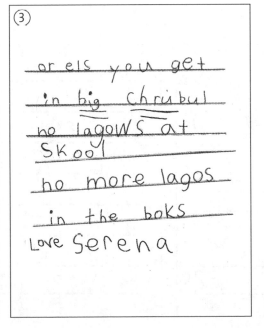

FIG. 2–2   Serena's letter

"Serena, you see how you reread this and *more* ideas came to your mind? You thought, 'If people don't do this, then. . . .' Whenever you are trying to persuade people to do something, you can do just what you just did! Reread your writing to get yourself to say more and try thinking to yourself 'This is important because . . .' This time, you said that to yourself and ended up thinking, 'Yeah! This is important because if kids don't do this then there's only Play-doh at Choice Time.'

"Serena, one more thing. Will you think about all that you have learned over this whole year, and think about what a writer like you should do after you have thought about all these other reasons why kids should bring back the Legos they've taken?"

"Add it?" Serena said. She looked back at her letter to the children and pointed to show that she was already at the bottom of the page and then clapped her hand over her mouth as if to convey, "I know! I know what to do!" and skipped off to the writing center to retrieve another page. As she headed off, I asked her to bring a whole bunch of add-on slips as well because I was quite sure that Serena's efforts would be infectious, leading others to try adding to their drafts. Upon her return, Serena added:

> or else you get in big trouble. No Legos at school, No more Legos
> in the box.

I restated what I hoped Serena would transfer to other pieces of writing, speaking in a way that made today's work as transferable as possible. "Serena, remember that whenever you are writing to convince people to help you, you are the kind of writer who includes an 'or else' as a way to tell your reader what *could happen* if the problem doesn't get fixed. Do this work in all your opinion writing." I then called for the attention of the writers at Serena's table and gave them a quick overview of the work Serena had done, which they could all do. Because Serena was a particularly proficient writer, I made the strategy seem especially accessible as I described it.

Of course, you'll help the novice writer have access to similar work doing this work with more supports. As you move among your students, conferring and leading small groups, be aware that your more novice writers can also profit from your help adding reasons to convince readers that the action they advocate is worthy, although some of the added content might be contained in speech bubbles. Perhaps in the drawing that accompanies the text, someone might say, "You better do this or else . . . " and fill in the consequence. Of course, this content can also be added into the text itself.

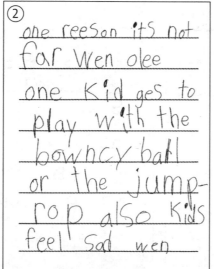
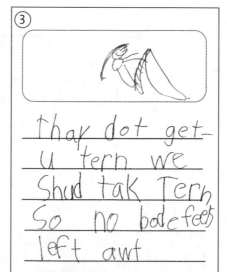

FIG. 2–3   Sofia includes reasons and consequences in speech and thought bubbles in her drawing and in the body of her letter.

Sharing Strategies to Make Your Writing Convincing

Channel children to reread their writing, identifying and talking about places where they tried to convince people, highlighting what they did that others could try.

"Writers, it is hard for me to believe that we have only been working for a few days on writing to convince people. You guys are becoming so convincing. Right now, will you meet with your partner? Partner 1, will you show your partner all the things you did in your writing so that you could convince people to really, really listen to you? Put your writing between the two of you, and read it closely. You might even put a star on parts you tried to convince people. Who knows? You and your partner could even get ideas today about how to make those parts even *more* convincing!"

Children talked. After a few minutes, I said, "You all came up with ideas I never even imagined. For example, a few of you added not only speech bubbles but also thought bubbles to show what characters will be thinking. Jack added thought bubbles to show, in his poster, what people will think if you all don't start putting your books away. And he showed what *kids* will think as well. Kids will think, 'I can't find any good books,' because all the books will be on the floor."

Then I said, "Jack may end up learning from Sofia because she first added speech bubbles and thought bubbles to her drawings, but then she went a step farther and added that writing to her actual sentences." I displayed Sofia's book and pointed first to some speech bubbles in her picture. I said to the children, "On this page (see Figure 2–3), Sofia, who is writing about recess, shows what will happen if nobody shares. One person in her picture is *saying* something: 'Recess is boring.' And one is thinking something: 'No fair.'" Then I pointed to the passage under the picture and said, "Look, Sofia made sure to pull those ideas down into her sentences." I read:

> Dear Ms. S,
> All the kids should share toys at recess or else it feels boring. One reason is it's not fair when
> only one kid gets to play with the bouncy ball or the jump rope. Also, kids feel sad when they
> don't get a turn. We should take turns so nobody feels left out. Recess is more fun! Love, Sofia

"Do you notice how Sofia's words are talking right to her reader? She used her ideas from her picture to give *lots* of reasons and *lots* of sentences so she can tell her reader exactly what she's thinking and what she wants her reader to do. You could try that in your writing, too."

Don't Stop There! Generating More Writing for More Causes

IN THIS SESSION, you'll teach students that opinion writers cast a wide net when writing, writing in a variety of genres and to a variety of audiences.

GETTING READY

✔ Chart paper and marker (see Teaching)

✔ "Writers Write to Make the World Better!" chart, from Session 1, revised (see Teaching)

✔ Class piece of shared writing, from previous session (see Teaching)

✔ "Writers Can Make a . . . " chart (see Teaching)

✔ Audio recording of "If I Had a Hammer" by Pete Seeger or other song that calls people to action (see Share)

✔ Excerpt of song lyrics, copied onto chart paper or displayed (see Share)

TEACHERS, now is not the time to slow down, leading your students one step at a time through your detailed image of exactly what you want them to produce. You are not after perfection. Instead, now is the time to create a buzzing energy. You'll want children to create lots of texts that rally readers for different causes. Imagine each child creating a folder-full of writing that is meant to change the world, and imagine children combing through their folders often, inserting some new technique into many of the texts.

It often helps to provide kids with examples, showing them ways other writers in the world have used words to petition for change. You might decide to play excerpts of well-known songs, such as Pete Seeger's "We Shall Overcome" or "If I Had a Hammer." Other possibilities are "We Are the World" by Michael Jackson or "Imagine" by John Lennon. Perhaps, you'll show photographs of signs and posters, held high during a protest rally. You might even read aloud Dr. Seuss's *The Lorax*, to liken the work that your children are doing to the hopeful petition of the Lorax, himself. Don't feel as if all of this needs to be contained within your writing workshop. Instead, you can start your whole day off with a read-aloud that helps to wrap youngsters in a feeling that they are embarking on some big and consequential work. You may worry that your kindergartners will never write in ways that mirror the compelling nature of these mentors, but understand that this launch is less about the product and much more about the underlying drive of the unit—words can change the world—and about communicating to kindergartners, "Your words matter."

COMMON CORE STATE STANDARDS: W.K.1, RL.K.1, RL.K.2, RL.K.3, RL.K.10, RI.K.8, SL.K.1, SL.K.2, L.K.1, L.K.2, L.K.6

Don't Stop There! Generating More Ideas and Writing for Many Causes

CONNECTION

Tell writers that they remind you of the Lorax, and retell the story of how he cares so much about trees that he tries to convince everyone to care for them.

"Writers, you've been doing some important work this week. You are using your words to help make things better in our classroom and in our school. A bunch of you will start your third, fourth, or even your fifth piece of writing today! And you're making so many different kinds of writing, too! Letters, songs, petitions, speeches, so many different ways to persuade others to help make things in our classroom and school better. Michael, can you come up here and sing your hand-washing song for us?" Michael proudly came to the front of the room, song in hand, and sang out loudly to the tune of "Jingle Bells" espousing for all the importance of hand washing (see Figure 3–1).

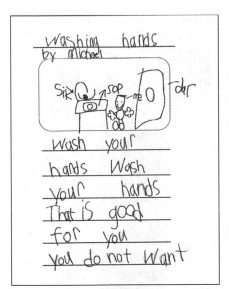
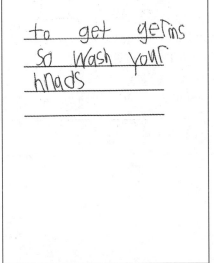

Wash your hands, Wash your hands, That is good for you, You do not want to get germs, So wash your hands

FIG. 3–1   Michael's song

Michael Fullan, who is perhaps the most prominent authority on school change, has said that the problem of changing schools comes down to one word: motivation. The problem of supporting writing development may also come down to that same one word. The old saying "Practice makes perfect" is not, actually, true. The truth is that "Perfect practice makes perfect." This means that for children to outgrow themselves as writers, it is important for them to work diligently to outgrow their own best efforts and to do this often. That comes down to a single word: motivation. We need to make sure we are encouraging kids' zeal.

"Each one of you reminds me of the Lorax, from Dr. Seuss's book. I know you all know about the Lorax, who saw that all the beautiful trees were getting chopped down. He cared so much about what was happening to his trees that he did all he could to convince everyone to care about them, too. He says in the story, 'Unless someone like you cares a whole awful lot, nothing is going to get better. It's not.'"

I read the quote that I had written on chart paper. Now, as I reread it once more, I pointed and invited the children to chime in. Then I turned back to the class, waited until the room was absolutely quiet, and said, "We need to listen to the Lorax. He's telling us something very important." I leaned in to whisper these words of advice. "If we want things to change, then we have to really, really care and we have to help make it better, or else these problems will never go away.

"You can use writing to convince people to make things better just like these writers did."

❧ **Name the teaching point.**

"Today I want to teach you that opinion writers don't just write one thing and say 'Oh, well. I hope that helps, but it is not my business.' No way. Instead, they keep writing more and more to tackle the problem they've seen. They write to different people, in different ways, and suggest different solutions. They keep at it."

TEACHING

Refer back to the previous day's chart and lesson, revising both to say that writers work on a lot of writing to address problems in the world.

"I think we need to change the chart we made the other day, because although it is true that we get ideas by seeing a problem, thinking of a way to fix it, and writing something to make it better, the truth is that to change the world, people don't just write *something*. People write *a lot* of things. Like that Lorax, who keeps trying and trying to convince people to take care of trees, writers try and try to find ways to fix the problems in the world.

"So I think we need to change our chart."

> Writers Write to Make the World Better!
>
> **We care a whole awful lot, just like the Lorax!**
>
> 1. See a problem.
>
> 2. Think.
>
> 3. Write a lot!

Many things about this teaching point should be familiar. To highlight the positive, we juxtapose it with the negative. To teach children ways that writers think, we literally put words to their mouths (or actually to their minds).

Recruit children to join you in considering kinds of writing (other than a book) that could address the issue under consideration, and then take the lead in generating possible genre.

"I've been working on that book about the problem in the hallway." I held up a chart-paper book and, turning the pages, I read it to the class.

> I think the hallways could be better because some people run.
>
> Kids should stop running, <u>or else</u> someone might fall down.
>
> They might hit their head on the wall and get bumps or bruises.
>
> Or kids could crash into each other!

"Hmm, what *else* could we write to make the hallways safer?" I paused to think, tapping my chin as I considered the options. "You already helped write a book about this, but some people might not see the book, so I am wondering how else we can use writing to make sure the problem gets fixed."

"We could make a big poster and hang it up in the halls. Or I could convince one of you to sing, and we could be like Pete Seeger and make a song about this to convince kids to stop running. Hmm. What else?"

A child called out "A letter?" and I snatched up the suggestion. "Great idea! Yes, I think I'll write a letter. I'm hoping you'll help. It will be a letter to all the kids in the school. Then we can send it to every class to make sure every kid knows about this problem."

Name what you just did in a way that makes the work you've taught and demonstrated transferable to the children's own writing and replicable another day.

"Writers, did you see how I didn't just write one thing about the problem? Instead, we thought, 'What *else* could I write to help fix this problem?' We thought about the other possible kinds of writing," I said and started to list possibilities, recording kinds that children called out as well as ones I knew.

"If you come up with other things that writers might make to fix a problem, we'll add them to this list."

ACTIVE ENGAGEMENT

Ask the children to reflect on the writing they have already done and then nudge them to go a step further and imagine another text they could make to address the same problem in a different way.

"Writers, close your eyes and think about one of the topics you have already written about or about one of the problems you have already seen in our classroom or school. When you have that topic in mind, open your eyes." Once all eyes were open, I continued.

In a subsequent minilesson you'll demonstrate adding information by using a revision strip dangling from the edge of the page. You'll explain that you used that extra slip of paper when there was no room on the page. It will help, therefore, if you cut the chart paper pages in your book so that the text fills the place on the pages for writing.

Children will be jumping onto their knees and calling, "I know, I know" and perhaps even calling out suggestions. This is as it should be. It suggests they are doing the very work you are about to demonstrate, doing that work alongside you. So the only thing is that you need to gesture, "Wait, wait, let me do this myself." That will allow you to demonstrate.

"Okay, writers. Tell your partner about one of the problems that you have been trying to fix. Go!"

The children talked for just half a minute before I voiced over the hubbub, saying, "Now tell your partner the kind of writing you already made—a letter, a sign, a song, a petition, a list—and tell your partner another kind of writing you think you *could* make to fix that problem."

I listened in and Christian said, "I already wrote a letter to Ms. Barton (see Figure 3–2)." He explained to his partner, "I said that she needed to help kids use 1–2 voices instead of 3–4–5 ones. Kids are too loud. They're gonna get in trouble."

Kimani, Christian's partner, said, "How 'bout writing to the kids, so they knew that they could get in trouble for using 3–4–5 voices?"

When Christian dismissed the idea, saying he had already written one letter, so no, he didn't think another letter made sense, I intervened to support the idea that often writers need to write tons of letters. "That Lorax didn't just try to convince one person to save the trees, did he? You are going to be as determined as the Lorax."

Meanwhile, a nearby group of children was talking about getting swings for the schoolyard. "It would be more fun with more stuff to play," Paul said. I whispered to Jacob that he needed to ask his partner what he'd be writing next to fix the problem. "I dunno," Paul said. "A song?" The two boys were soon strumming on air guitars and composing verses about swings.

Convene the class and share some children's ideas as a way to help others generate ideas.

I convened the class. "So the other day Paul wrote a letter to the principal that started like this, 'Dear Ms. S, Can we put swings outside so we can have fun at recess?' Now, guess what he plans to write?"

Some children called out guesses, and I nodded that those were all good suggestions and then turned to Paul, who announced that he was going to write a song and did a quick rendition on the spot.

LINK

List the various options children will be pursuing, highlighting the fact that writers don't just write one kind of text to address a problem they see in the world.

"So, writers, today some of you will be finishing the writing you began the other day. And sometime today, most of you will start another piece of writing about the same problem. Give me a thumbs up if you think you might look at our list of kinds of writing to give yourself an idea." Many signaled. I added, "Some of you will be writing about a whole new problem. Remember that *anytime* you feel like you're ready to start a new piece, you can look around again and think, 'What *else* do I see that could be better?' Then decide, 'What can I write to fix it?' That way, you'll show the Lorax that there are *many* things you want to make better."

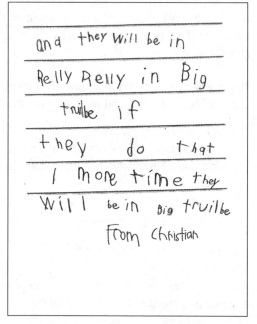

FIG. 3–2   Christian already wrote this letter to his teacher Ms. Barton, and now makes plans to write to kids.

Taking Stock of Your Writing Workshop by Altering the Lens with Which You Observe

I FIND THAT IT HELPS ME to approach a day's writing workshop with some main goals, because otherwise it is very easy to fall into ruts, doing the same thing day after day. Since the start of the unit, my interactions with kids had mostly been aimed toward luring them into the work that I taught during that day's minilesson or the preceding day's minilesson. Today I wanted to deliberately do something different.

There is a quote from Proust over my desk. "The real art of discovery consists not in finding new lands but in seeing with new eyes." That quote helps me to remember that we do not see with our eyes or hear with our ears, but with our minds. I can look at children in the midst of writing workshop and see only the extent to which they are complying with the request in that day's minilesson, or I can choose to alter the lens through which I look.

MID-WORKSHOP TEACHING   Writers Don't Stop—and Partners Help Writers Keep Going

I stood in the middle of the room to signal for the students to take a break in their writing and look up at me. "Writers, I want to commend you on the important work you've been doing this week. You are using your words in ways that will help not just you, but lots of people. This is all very impressive and grown-up. But I want to remind you that you can't stop—even when you feel like you're all done. You need to keep going!

"Can I share with you something so smart that Gabi and Lindsay just did together?" The girls smiled proudly, thrilled to be complimented in front of the group. "Gabi was concerned by how many books are in our Book Hospital box because they are torn, so she thought we needed to all be more careful with our books. So she wrote this letter" (see Figure 3–3).

> Ms. Rios
>
> Please remind K-139 to take a lot more care of the books. If you have a lot
> of trouble if you want I can help you.

"Lindsay suggested she could write more things about the problem, like a sign for the wall of our library, so Gabi plans to do that next. That's what writers do! They look back at their old writing to look for ideas for new writing! So, writers, when it feels hard to keep going, work with your partner to share new ideas for what else you could make." Then I said, "Right now, will you sit closely beside your partner,

and will Partner 2 put your folder between you and share the writing you've already done? Then together, will you try to make a plan for the writing Partner 2 can do next? Then, you can switch!"

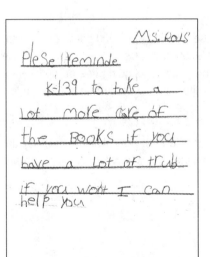

FIG. 3–3   Gabriella's letter

For example, I find it helpful to realize that when I am watching a writing workshop, I can choose to watch through the lens of independence, noting the extent to which children can work with independence on a project of their own choosing. If I look at their work with this lens, I start by recognizing that I'm not just considering their abilities to write, I'm also studying their abilities to work on their own steam for forty-five minutes. I can scan then, to note the varied levels of engagement in the work.

Of course, whatever lens one uses will reveal challenges that can then be addressed in conferences, small groups, mid-workshop teaching, shares, and/or minilessons. If I look with the lens of noticing student engagement, for example, I might notice that kids who seem especially involved have already recruited some others to join them, with a whole table full of youngsters writing signs and letters and books about a shared problem. Presto! That gives me an idea for future direction for the unit. Or perhaps I see that kids who are particularly engaged are working with new kinds of materials—poster paper, tiny notepads, greeting cards. Again, this leads me to sense a direction I could suggest to the class.

When you step back to study your classroom, chances are good that some children will seem to be at a standstill and others will be off-task. If I'm still looking with the lens of engagement, I might ask myself, "What are the different reasons I am seeing for disengagement?"

Why Might Kids Be Off-Task

◆ Some children might be off task because this kind of writing doesn't take them long. They state the problem and the solution in a sentence or two. So while narratives and informational writing provided an ongoing line of work—(the bit-by-bit story continues), it takes very little time to produce at least a modest version of this new job. Then kids feel "done."

◆ Some kids might be off task because they do not really know what they are supposed to do. In other units, the message was more clear. During *Small*

Moments they were asked to write a true story, touching the pages of the book first and saying the story aloud. The *How-To Books* unit was equally straight forward. Now there are more choices.

◆ Some kids may be off task because they do best when they can move around. It's spring, and they are wiggly.

Once I can think about the various reasons for a problem, I can think about the solutions, and this will probably lead to small-group work designed to help. With the first group, for example, I could gather a small group and point out they are writing too little. I could show them Maura's petition, which we'd studied earlier, and ask them to count the number of reasons she provides for why there needs to be a dog park, and I could challenge the kids to provide an equal number of reasons in their writing. I could ask kids to work with each other to see if they can push to more reasons than they ever dreamt possible.

In the same way, I could gather a small group of students who struggle with disengagement. Perhaps that group seems to require more direction and fewer choices. Perhaps I need to perk things up. Should I suggest then, writers work with marker pens and chart paper—a surefire engaging activity? Should I recruit them to spend a bit of time posting their writing around the school? My point is not so much to describe solutions to every imaginable challenge as to point out that it is important to deliberately choose to look at the class in different ways that then allow you to see different things. If one day I choose to look at engagement and to address ways to promote more engagement, another day I could look carefully at the role partners are playing and ways to make those partnerships more powerful. Or I could look at the ways students are using the charts from this unit and earlier units to help them plan their work for the day. Best of all, the teacher needn't be the only one to look through one lens or another. Youngsters, too, can be part of this process of taking stock and imagining next steps.

Studying a Mentor Text
Social Action Songs

Channel children to listen to a social action song, perhaps one with a refrain, and to use that song as a mentor text, noticing what the author did to make the song persuasive.

"Writers, during our lesson, I told you about Pete Seeger, who looked around and decided to write songs about the problems he saw. He used singing to help people understand these problems and help him fix things to make the world better. Right now, let's listen to one of his famous songs. The name of this song is 'If I Had a Hammer.' As you listen, think about the parts that stand out the most or the parts you really like." I played an excerpt of the song.

I faded the song out after the second verse and prompted the students to turn and share their thoughts.

"Now, let's look closely at some parts of the song." I displayed an excerpt of the lyrics, the two stanzas using a hammer and a bell. "As you sing it with me, think about what Pete did as a songwriter to convince people to help him that you might try, too." I invited the students to read along with me.

Convene the class to share observations about the text—the song—they have studied, making sure that you help them name what worked in ways that are applicable to other texts on other topics.

"What do you notice about this song? What do you notice Pete decided to do in his song that you might try in your own writing?"

"It's like the same thing over and over. Like hammer, hammer, hammer. Three times!" Jaden noticed.

"So, you noticed that Pete used repetition. He repeated words again and again," I echoed back.

Debrief in ways that communicate the transferable nature of students' observations.

"Hmm, those are smart ideas. The repetition makes it sound a lot more like a song. And if people can remember the words easily, they'll all be able to sing along. Maybe that way, they'll help him fix the problem. You might decide to try that in your writing, too!" I went on to elicit several other responses from students. Then I added, "So, writers, remember, when you want to find ways to make your writing even better, it helps to look at what other writers in the world have done. You can look, or listen closely, and think, 'What did this writer do that I could try, too?'"

As students share their observations, you may choose to list them as transferable strategies for song writing on chart paper.

Writers Reread and Fix Up Their Writing

IN THIS SESSION, you'll teach students that writers do not wait for others to tell them how to revise their writing. They reread what they have written and think, "What can I do to make my writing better?"

GETTING READY

✔ Excerpt of song lyrics from previous session, copied onto chart paper or projected in the class (see Connection)

✔ New and improved "When We Are Done, We've Just Begun" chart, originally created in *Launching the Writing Workshop* unit (see Teaching)

✔ Demonstration writing from Sessions 2 and 3 (see Teaching)

✔ Revision strips, to use during the minilesson and also for your students to use during independent writing time (see Teaching)

✔ Tape (see Teaching)

✔ Student writing folders (see Active Engagement)

✔ Post-it® notes (see Active Engagement)

✔ Student writing sample to model revising across many pages (see Mid-Workshop Teaching)

✔ White boards and dry erase markers for each student (see Share)

COMMON CORE STATE STANDARDS: W.K.1, W.K.5, W.1.1, RFS.K.1, RFS.K.2, RFS.K.3, SL.K.1, SL.K.2, SL.K.3, SL.K.4, SL.K.5, L.K.1, L.K.2

TODAY, instead of teaching brand-new content, you'll teach children to draw on all they have already learned to make decisions about how to make their writing better. Your students will have been taught many general revision strategies across the year. They've learned that writers can tip their "magic pencils" around and tap at each word with the eraser end of the pencil. They've learned to tape revision strips onto their writing when they find they still have more to say. They know they can reread, thinking, "What questions will my readers have?" and then revise to anticipate those questions. Now is a good time to do the more encompassing work of reminding them that they can bring *all they know* about revision and editing to the work they are doing in this new unit. Researchers have shown repeatedly that transference does not happen without explicit attention.

So often, young writers wait for the teacher to signal their every move. "Help! What do I do next? I'm done!" they say to us. This session is your reply. You answer, "You don't need *me* to tell you what to do next. No way! You know so many ways to make your writing the best it can be. Don't wait! Reread, and decide what to do." Your message is, "*You* are the boss during writing workshop, not me. *You* decide what you'll do to make your writing better."

This won't be the first time you have reminded children to reread their writing with pen in hand, evaluating what they have done, noticing what needs work, and then diving in to fix things. So watch what children do in the name of rereading and revising. Explain that instead of telling them what to do, you will be a researcher, observing the choices they make. You'll probably see that most of your students still equate revisions and editing with an effort to ferret out errors. Of course, the scale of the errors that children see will differ—some will find pictures that don't yet have labels and pages that don't yet have words and others will spot sentences that are unclear.

Of course, it won't just be the children who study the situation and then decide what to do. You'll do that as well. You could decide to teach any one of an array of things. For example, you could tell kids that you notice that most of them think of revision as fixing mess-ups, but that many grown-up professional writers think of revision as a time to try things another way. Of course you'd then point out that writers who revise in order to try another way may end up looking back at the different options to choose which is best. That means that a writer might notice that her letter about not running in the halls starts with a ques-

"In this session, your message is, 'You are the boss during writing workshop, not me. You decide what you'll do to make your writing better."

tion and might think "What else could I have tried?" and then that writer might consider other ways to start her writing. A whole pile of questions? A story? A fact? A sound word?

Then again, if you decided to tell children that you notice they are revising by fixing mess ups, you could then point out that pro writers instead tend to revise by finding the best parts of a piece of writing and thinking "How can I do more writing that is as good as this best part?"

Or you could tell children that writers revise by looking at what someone else did—a published writer or a friend, saying "I could try that."

You could also teach writers that it is helpful to use partners as revision and editing supports.

You might then teach listening partners to read closely and give specific compliments and suggestions. Partners might say, "I like the way you . . . ," and then they can cite particular lines and elaborate about why those lines are especially notable. Partners could also say "I wonder why you . . ." and again cite specifics.

All of these, then, are ways to support revision and editing.

Writers Reread and Fix Up Their Writing

CONNECTION

Tweak the song children listened to in the preceding session so that it celebrates writing to change the world.

"I was thinking about that Pete Seeger song we listened to yesterday and thinking that our class is not using hammers and bells to signal danger, to let out a warning. Instead we are using writing—letters and signs and songs and petitions. So I wonder if we could change the words of that song so that it becomes a song about our writing? Let's listen to it again and think about whether we could change the words.

"How could we change it?" Children chimed in, and soon we were singing this.

If I had an opinion

I'd write in the morning

I'd write in the evening

All over this land

I'd write out danger

I'd write out a warning

I'd help fix the problems

All over this land

This will not be the first time that you engaged children in singing as a way to convene the minilesson. In Unit 2, children studied vowels by altering the refrain of "Old MacDonald." In both instances, I can't help but think, "Yes!" Hopefully you and your children will find yet more ways to bring song, dance, art, and drama into minilessons. Send us your ideas!

❖ Name the teaching point.

"Today I want to teach you that writers don't wait around for someone else to tell them how to make their writing better—or in this case how to make their writing more persuasive, more convincing. Writers reread what they have written and think, 'How can I make this even better?' Then they change their writing, without anyone telling them what to do. Writers are the bosses of their own writing."

You are going all out to recruit your youngsters' passion. "Writers don't wait around for someone else to tell them what to do. No way! Writers are the bosses of their writing." Play this up.

TEACHING

Remind children that they are in charge of their writing, so they need to make decisions about whether a piece is done for now or needs further revision.

"Writers, I want everyone to take a second, close your eyes, and time travel back to the very beginning of the school year, *way* back to September." I looked out at the students, noticing eyes closed and faces scrunched up with the effort of remembering all the way back. "Way back then, we spent a lot of time working on writing true stories from our lives. Do you remember that? As the year went on, we tried different kinds of writing. But no matter what kind of writing you have been doing, one thing always stays the same. You are the boss of your own writing. You are in charge. And being in charge of your writing means it is up to *you* to decide when you are done with your writing. It is not my decision to make. It's not your mom's decision. It's not your writing partner's decision. It is your decision.

"I want to show you something. Remember this? Remember our 'When We Are Done, We've Just Begun' chart? I've pulled it back out for us to use again, but now, I've made some changes. I've switched some things around and added to it, because you all know so much more now than you did way back in September. I've also added on some things that you can do to make your persuasive writing stronger. I'm going to read you the new and improved 'When We Are Done, We've Just Begun' chart." I pointed at the items on the chart as I read it aloud.

> ### When We Are Done, We've Just Begun
>
> We can . . .
>
> - Reread
> - Meet with partners
> - Add more drawings and labels
> - Fix up parts that are not easy to read
> - Tell more reasons
> - Give an "or else . . ."
> - Add speech bubbles

To build your students' repertoire across the year, think about ways to grow strategy charts from earlier units. In this example, the chart has been revised to include elaboration strategies that pertain to the work of the current unit, while maintaining and reinforcing applicable strategies learned at the start of the year.

"You can use this chart to help you decide whether you are done with your writing or whether you still have more work to do."

Recruit the class to join you in rereading the book you've written about a school problem, helping you consider how to make the text more persuasive. Then demonstrate the process of adding more reasons for addressing the problem.

"Let's use the 'When We Are Done, We've Just Begun' chart to help us figure out whether we are done with the book about running in the halls or if there is still more that we can do to make it better! The first thing we need to do is reread it." I retrieved the piece and read aloud from the beginning, pointing below each word to model careful inspection.

> I think the hallways could be better. The hall would be safer if people didn't run. Kids should stop running, or else someone might fall down. They might hit their head on the wall and get bumps and bruises. Or kids could crash into each other!

I stopped dramatically. "Hmm, I'm not sure that my writing is all that convincing yet. Let me take a look at our chart and see if that will help me figure out what to do." I read over the items on the chart, mumbling to myself, thinking aloud about what to do. "Wait! I got it! We can add to our words by telling more reasons. Yes! I think that is what this writing needs. Maybe I could add one more reason why people shouldn't run." I reread, grabbed a revision strip and wrote the following.

> If you run, you could fall on your face. Don't run!

I taped the new sentence strip to my book, letting it hang off the side of the page.

"Did you see what I did? I used a revision strip to add another sentence to my writing. There wasn't really any room on the page for me to squeeze another sentence in and still have my writing be readable. But my idea is really, really important. Just like when we were writing true stories and how-to books, we used revision strips, we can also use them in our persuasive writing, too!"

Reiterate what you have done in way that makes the process transferable to another day and another piece.

"Writers, you can do this, too. You are the boss of your own writing, and *you* decide what will make your pieces better. You can use the new and improved 'When We Are Done, We've Just Begun' chart to help you figure out what you can do to make your writing stronger or whether you are done and ready to move on to something new. The important thing is to reread often and ask, 'What can I do to make this better?' Then, using every little bit of what you know about writing, decide what your piece needs."

FIG. 4-1 Teacher demonstration writing before a flap containing another reason is added.

ACTIVE ENGAGEMENT

Recruit the children to reread their own writing, weighing ways to make it more persuasive.

"Are you ready to be the boss? Take out your writing folders and decide what you'll do right now to make your writing even better. Use the chart to help figure out what your writing might need." Students opened up their folders and pulled out pieces. I voiced over, "I notice that many of you are rereading. That's the smartest way to decide what your writing needs."

I crouched beside Jessica, who had reached the third page of her book. "Jessica, what might you do to make your writing even better?" She stared down at the page and shrugged. "Well, what do you already know about writing from this whole year in kindergarten that could help you with this book?"

She paused and then replied, "You need labels in the picture?"

I nodded. "That's right! And our chart says we can add more drawings or labels to our pictures. Is that something your piece might need?"

Jessica flipped back through her pages and pointed to her first picture box. "Yeah, right here there's only one. I think I can put more."

Channel children to Post-it places in their text that they could revise to make them more persuasive.

By now, it was time to talk to the class. "Writers, I'm going to pass out Post-its, and will you use these to mark places in your writing where you want to do some revision? Put the Post-it on all the spots where you plan to revise." After they did this, I suggested children tell their partners what they planned to do.

LINK

Rally children to take ownership of the process of rereading and fixing up their writing, listing several ways they know to make writing more persuasive.

"So from now on, remember, *you* are the one in charge when it comes to your writing. Don't wait for me or anyone else to tell you to reread or fix it up. The new and improved 'When We Are Done, We've Just Begun' chart can help you figure out how to revise your writing!"

Luring Children to Revise

I T IS IMPORTANT TO REALIZE that revision comes easily to kindergarten children and that it need not be a huge deal to lure five-year-olds to revise. After all, watch a child draw, and you are apt to see the child draw one thing and then continue drawing, so the picture becomes something different. In block play, too, what begins as a castle morphs into a hotel. The revisions that come early to young children do not always involve reflection, judgment, and plans. This may result from just a continual process of adding on. But revision is not a big deal for kindergarteners. Your children will have learned to do this in prior units, and you should expect that, without a doubt, they are revising often and with independence during this unit as well.

Of course, some children will be so eager to store a piece of writing in the "done" section of their folder and to launch into a new endeavor that they might declare a number of half-done pieces to be completed, so you'll remind them that every writer takes time often to look back on prior work and to think about ways to improve that work.

You might sit beside a child who is keen on starting a new piece and ask, "But wait! Before you go back to the writing center for more paper, will you take me on a tour of your whole folder? I'd love to see the work you've been doing so far. Which one is your best one yet?" When children are asked to be selective with their choices, they often do so with a more thoughtful eye. Because revision is not always a response to judgment, you might engage this writer in a conversation about what makes this piece better than the others. This could essentially ignite plans for improving other pieces to make them match the level of the writing the child identifies as his or her best. Granted, for a five-year-old this might mean making the pictures better before adding more sentences to persuade an audience. But, remember, this is a child who would otherwise skip back to the writing center without giving the piece of writing a second thought.

If you provide writers with revision, or fix-it-up, tools, you'll add allure to the revision process. Writers love being given scissors, tape, and brads so they can add revision strips and flaps and new pages to their drafts. You might even provide small sticky notes or speech bubble cutouts to encourage students to add more labels and dialogue in their writing.

MID-WORKSHOP TEACHING   Revising Across Every Page

"Writers," I began. "I need everyone's eyes up here." I paused, waiting for everyone to stop their writing and look up at me. "Sometimes when you've found a way to fix up one part of your book, it helps to look for other places in that piece of writing where you can try that same thing." I displayed a classmate's piece. "Check this out! Andrew realized this page in his book could use a speech bubble to show what the people are saying. Then he looked for other parts of his piece where he could have added speech bubbles, and wow! Those places were everywhere!" I continued to flip through Andrew's book, pointing out the many places Andrew had found to insert speech bubbles. "Isn't that terrific? After you find one part to revise, it's not time to simply say, 'All done!' and stop. You can search for *more* parts to fix up. You can even go back to finished pieces of writing and find yet more places to do that same work."

Stretching Words Out Like Rubber Bands

Champion one child who came to a tricky word and instead of pleading for help, stretched the word out like a rubber band.

After asking the children to bring dry erase materials to their spots in the meeting area, I sat down in my chair and called one of the students to sit beside me with her writing. Then I shared the work she did, all on her own. "Class, guess what your friend Bailee did today!" I paused and leaned in close, filling the students with anticipation. Then I whispered as if unraveling a gripping tale, "She needed a word—a super tricky word. First she checked the word wall, but it wasn't there! So, do you know what she did next? She stretched that word out so that she could write it the very best she could, all by herself. Not for one single minute did she think, 'Oh no! I'm stuck. Let me ask the teacher, for help.' No way! Instead, she said, 'I can do this!' and she stretched the word out like a long rubber band, until she wrote down every sound she could hear."

I turned to Bailee, who by this point was sitting proudly and smiling ear to ear. "Bailee, will you hold up the page where you worked on that tricky, tricky word. Point to that word that you spelled and read it to us."

Bailee held her writing up high and pointed to a word mid-sentence. "Permission," she read.

"*Permission*! That really is a tricky word, don't you think?" The class nodded with wide eyes, clearly impressed. "I bet you can do exactly what Bailee did to spell the trickiest of tricky words! Right now, pick up your dry erase tools and let's all try what Bailee did to spell another tricky word. How about the word *please*?" I coached in, using lean prompts as students worked individually to spell the word on their white boards. "Say the word out loud." "Stretch it long like a rubber band." "What do you hear? Write it." "Say it again. What do you hear next? Write it!"

Once students had finished spelling the word as best they could, I asked the group to raise their white boards up high and I celebrated their approximations. Then I restated the teaching point. "Writers spell tricky words the best they can so that readers can read them. Writers say the word as slowly as they can, stretching it out like a rubber band and listening to every sound they hear. As writers hear each sound, they write the letter down on the page."

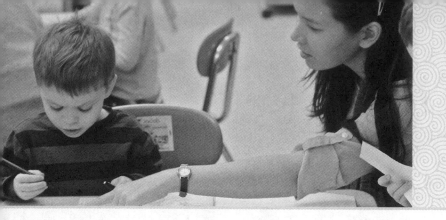

Spelling Strategies Give Writers Word Power

IN THIS SESSION, you'll teach students that writers call upon many strategies to figure out how to write words that are hard to spell.

GETTING READY

✔ White boards and dry erase markers for each student (see Connection, Active Engagement, and Share)

✔ Demonstration writing from Sessions 2, 3, and 4 (Bend I) (see Connection, Teaching)

✔ "Writers Don't Say 'How do You Spell?'" chart (see Teaching)

✔ "How to Turn a Word into a Snap Word" chart (see Conferring and Small-Group Work)

✔ Students' writing folders to select piece for publication (see Share)

COMMON CORE STATE STANDARDS: W.K.1, W.1.1, RFS.K.1, RFS.K.2, RFS.K.3, SL.K.1, L.K.1, L.K.2.c,d

L IKE THE LAST SESSION, this session does not teach children anything new. You won't teach a new strategy for spelling those hard words or a new way to remember sight vocabulary. Instead, today you'll remind your students that they already know how to help themselves get unstuck, because all year, they have been boosting their word power.

During this session, you'll talk to those writers in distress who continue to call out, "How do you spell . . . ?" You'll guide those students to recall the repertoire of strategies they have learned all year, deciding on which they will use to spell today's hard word the best they can, all on their own.

From time to time, and certainly during this session, you'll want to reference a classroom spelling strategy chart. Post the chart beside you in the meeting area, so that you can breathe new life into it and ensure that kids actively reference it across the year, the unit, and the day. Moving a chart into a premiere position serves to keep that chart alive in your classroom—that's important because charts support independence.

The Common Core State Standards ask that kindergartners "write a letter or letters for most consonant and short-vowel sounds (phonemes)" and "spell simple words phonetically, drawing on knowledge of sound-letter relationships." This certainly reflects the teaching you have done all year, helping your children listen for the sounds they hear in a word and then recording the letter that makes that sound. You've taught students to use alphabet charts and blends and digraph charts. You've reminded them to use the classroom word wall and to use personal word walls in their writing folders as well.

At the start of today's minilesson, you will ask children to name the strategies they know and use to spell. You'll celebrate the word power of your now much smarter, stronger, and more independent kindergartners. You'll say, "You don't need *me*, or anyone else, to help you figure out how to spell words, even hard words, because you have word power!" This sets you up to help students realize they already know so many ways to help themselves get unstuck.

In the minilesson, your students will use white boards to practice drawing from their repertoire of strategies. You'll coach them as they work methodically on words you present.

Your conferences and small-group work will need to be tailored to support the full range of levels within your class. Your novice spellers will need practice isolating sounds and identifying the letters that make those sounds. Your more proficient spellers may benefit from work with long vowel patterns or familiar word parts.

"Today you'll say, 'You don't need ME, *or anyone else, to help you figure out how to spell words, even the ones that are hard, because you have word power!'"*

You will end today's session with a share that is something of a drumroll leading up to the first mini-celebration of the unit. Students will reread the writing they have done to date and choose one piece to publish. Since this is just a mini-publishing, they will not have more than one session to get their writing ready to send out into the world.

Spelling Strategies Give Writers Word Power

CONNECTION

Act utterly helpless and needy over everything. You can't find your tools, you can't spell hard words.

As children came to the meeting area, I gave them dry erase boards and markers, asking them to sit on the boards until later. Once the children were seated in their rug spots, I approached the meeting area. I paused dramatically at the foot of the rug. I let out a sigh and scratched my head. "Where do I go now?" The students giggled and pointed to my chair beside the easel. "Oh!" I walked over and sat down. I looked around my chair and shrugged, "I need a marker. I don't have a marker! Now what?"

Again, the class giggled at my helpless act, and Jack called out, "Get one from the marker bucket!"

"Oh, thanks Jack." I got myself a marker. I opened up my writing folder and took out a book I'd been writing. I pointed to a part of my drawing and explained, "This is the bookshelf. Let me label it." I began to write a label alongside the picture. I furrowed my brow and whined, "I don't know how to spell *bookshelf*! That's too hard!"

Arms shot up to help me.

When children suggest there are ways to figure out a hard word, act persuaded, and turn this into a lesson on the importance of being a resourceful problem solver. Collect suggestions for how to solve the hard word.

Looking astonished at the idea that there were solutions at hand, I said, "What? You guys have suggestions for ways I could help myself?" When the children called out that yes, they could help, I nodded and changed my role, as if persuaded. Sitting tall, assuming a position of more active agency, I said, "You are right. I don't have to be whiny, needy, and helpless, do I? I might not know *everything*, but there are ways I can figure things out.

"So let's work together to figure out how I could go about trying to spell *bookshelf*." Students turned to partners as I listened in to their suggestions. I heard students offer, "Check the word wall." "Look right there," pointing to a label on the bookshelf in the library. "Stretch it out."

Nodding, I said, "I heard so many smart ways I could figure this out by myself. If I tap you, will you say out loud what you think I should do?" One by one, I tapped on the shoulders of students who named spelling strategies the class had learned to use so far that year.

When I'm role-playing the part of a needy student, I always think of that old-fashioned song "In a cabin in the woods, a little old man by the window stood. Saw a rabbit hopping by, knocking at his door. 'Help me, help me' the rabbit said . . . " When I sang that song as a little girl, I always threw my hands up in an utterly needy way, and the "help me" was especially squeaky and desperate. So now, when trying to dramatize the sort of stance I hope writers do not take, I become that little rabbit in the woods, whimpering, "Help me, help me." This time, I add, "I need a marker, oh dear, oh dear." But the point is not the marker. The point is that in life, every one of us has a choice. We can be high-maintenance people, needing others to solve our every problem, or we can be independent, resourceful problem solvers. The choice is a very big deal.

It may seem to you that we've forgotten that this is a unit on persuasive writing, allowing ourselves to get consumed by the challenges of getting anything at all on the page. Although we aren't talking and writing about persuasive writing, this is what youngsters are doing every day. They haven't forgotten.

Reinforce the larger point that children need to be self-reliant problem solvers to spell hard words and to solve other challenges.

"This year in kindergarten, you have been growing in so many ways. You're getting taller. Your muscles are getting stronger. You're learning tons. You are all bigger and taller and stronger and smarter, and you don't need to say, 'Help me! Help me!' anymore, like I was saying before. You can figure things out by yourselves. You don't have to say," and I leaned over and tugged on Kevin's shirt as I whined, "How do you spell . . . ? because you know so many ways to spell the best you can."

❖ **Name the teaching point.**

"Today I want to teach you that even when words are hard, writers don't say 'Help me! Help me!' Instead, writers think about all the ways they know how to write words. Then they decide which strategies they will use to spell the best they can."

TEACHING

Collect strategies for spelling hard words, and then demonstrate using those strategies.

"I want to write *basket* but it's not on our word wall and it is HARD. Hmm . . ." I said. "Oh! I know. I will use our strategies to spell it. Watch how I use all those strategies to do this hard job." I pointed to a chart where I had already listed the spelling strategies students had learned.

"B-basket. I hear /b/ at the start of the word. Let me write that sound down." I recorded the initial sound and proceeded. "Let me stretch it out and listen for more sounds." I gestured with my hands as if I were stretching the physical word. "B-ask-it." I repeated it again slowly. "I need a vowel, and I hear /a/. Let me add that vowel next."

I continued through the word, this time with an emphasis on the blend. "/sk/ That's a sound I know. Oh! I see it on that chart." I pointed to a blends chart in the room. "*S* and *k* make /sk/, like in *skunk*. Let me write those letters next." I returned to the word, sliding my finger across the recorded sounds. "Wait, I hear a little word that I know at the end— *it*! I know how to spell that word. It's on the word wall!" I quickly recorded the ending. Then I pointed below my label and read, "The trash *baskit*."

Debrief in ways that restate the teaching point and remind children to draw on their growing repertoire of spelling strategies.

I turned to address the class, "Did you see how I did that? I used everything I know to spell the word all by myself." I counted the strategies used across my fingers as I named them aloud. "I checked the word wall. I stretched the word out like a rubber band so I could hear a lot of sounds. I remembered to include a vowel. I even used a chart in the room to help me with some of those sounds. I didn't ask anyone to help me, because I know a lot of strategies to spell the best I can."

ACTIVE ENGAGEMENT

Coach children to spell a challenging word on their white boards, using all the strategies in their repertoire.

"Now let's all try it! Let's use everything we know to spell words all by ourselves." I pointed to another part of my drawing. "I need to label this water fountain. Think about all the strategies you know to spell *fountain* without asking for help!" I coached writers to try a repertoire of strategies to spell independently and voiced over reminders to check the spelling chart.

Debrief in ways that highlight the transferable strategies you hope children use often.

I stopped the class and prompted them to reflect on their process. "Now, will you think about everything you had to do to spell this word by yourself? Use your fingers to teach your partner what strategies you tried." I listened in as partners named back what they did and prompted struggling students to look at the class chart again to figure out which strategy they tried to help them spell.

You'll notice that the word students are asked to spell is very challenging. This is intentional, so that students are required to problem solve using a repertoire of strategies to spell. Remember, the goal is not to spell this word correctly, but instead to encourage children to be independent word solvers.

You debrief by highlighting the strategies children used, not the correct spelling.

LINK

Repeat the teaching point, and send children off to work.

"So from now on, writers, any time you feel stuck on a tricky word, instead of saying, 'Help me! Help me! How do you spell . . . ?' think about all the strategies you know for spelling the best you can on your own. This way, you can get stronger and more independent as writers. If you forget some of our spelling strategies, look back at the chart! Because if you want your writing to persuade others to take action, they need to be able to read it. Ready writers? Let's get writing!"

You'll want to use actions to accompany both the ready pose and the self-reliant one. Perhaps you'll throw your hands up in despair when ready, and show your muscles when self-reliant.

Differentiating Instruction in the Use of the Word Wall

YOUR CONFERENCES AND SMALL-GROUP WORK provide you with the opportunity to teach children spelling strategies that are targeted to their specific needs. For instance, some writers will benefit from you reminding them to check the word wall for high-frequency words instead of stretching and recording sounds for those words. On the other hand, there will be other writers who have no problem referencing the word wall and who, in fact, seem to do that *too* often. After all, after a while, the whole point is for the words on the word wall to become words that children "just know in a snap," for sight words to become automatic.

So there will be some writers who will benefit from lessons in how to actually *learn* the spelling of those word wall words. You could say to these writers, "It helps to look at the word carefully, take a picture of it in your mind and then, write the word without looking at the word wall, spelling it the way you remember. And then, check it!" You could draw their attention back to an anchor chart from the *Writing for Readers* unit you taught earlier in the year.

say, "Remember, whenever you know a word in a snap, you don't need to waste time getting up and walking over to the word wall. Close your eyes and picture the word wall—and the word!—in your mind. Then write it fast, all by yourself. But if that word is still a bit tricky, and you can't see it when you close your eyes, check the word wall afterward to help you." This might be a great time to leave behind an index card with this strategy, abbreviating your teaching in a way that will remind this writer to do this always.

Of course, your conferring will not target spelling alone. The challenge when writing is that writers need, above all, to multitask. The act of writing requires that writers think about genre, purpose, audience, content, craft, process, and convention, using an executive function to shift from thinking about one of these things to thinking about another. On a day when the minilesson focused exclusively on spelling, it will be especially important that your conferring and small-group work remind children to continue to draw on all they know, not just spelling strategies.

How to Turn a Word into a Snap Word

1. Look at it carefully.

2. Take a picture of it.

3. Write it.

4. Check it!

After you have reminded the class or a small group of children of the process that writers go through to learn by heart the words on the word wall, you could say to any one writer, "I bet you know that word without even needing to check the wall! Let's see if you can write it all by yourself, without the word wall helping you." You might

---

MID-WORKSHOP TEACHING   Spellers Are Resourceful, Using the Classroom for Support

I stood in the middle of the room and asked for writers' attention. "Writers, spellers, remember, when you are trying to spell a word and you have that 'Oh no! I'm stuck' feeling, you can use the classroom as a helper. Look around you right now and point to a place in the classroom that might help you spell a tricky word." Outstretched arms pointed in zigzags across the room. I narrated what I saw. "That's right. You can use the charts hanging up, the blends poster or the word walls in the room. Jessica even pointed to the tools inside her writing folder. You can use your personal word wall or the ABC chart to help you do your best, all by yourselves. That way, when you're feeling stuck, you can figure the tricky word out without saying, 'How do you spell . . . ?'"

Selecting a Piece for the Mini-Celebration

Guide students to reread the writing they have done thus far, selecting one piece for the upcoming mini-celebration.

"Writers, I have some very exciting news for you. Tomorrow you will get a chance to get your ideas, your opinions, out into the world! Remember, if you want people to change, to help you solve the problems that you are seeing, you need to get your ideas out there! Your job right now will be to read through the pieces in your folder and choose the one you'd like to publish tomorrow. Don't worry if it's not quite done, not quite ready to send out into the world. You will have time tomorrow to finish it up and get it ready to share. So take a few minutes right now to read through your writing and select the piece you want to publish. I'll come around to give you a hand if you need one."

As I made my way around the meeting area, I noticed Jack sitting with two pieces (see Figures 5–1 and 5–2) in front of him, his face scrunched up, clearly deep in thought. He looked up at me and, before I could say a word, picked up

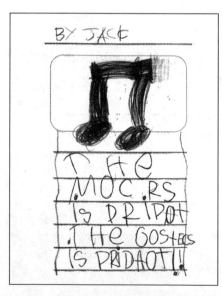

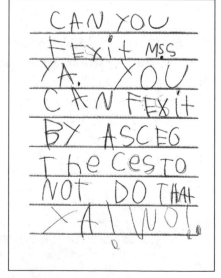

The markers is dried out. The glue sticks is dried out! Can you fix it Ms. S? Yeah. You can fix it by asking the kids to not do that. Ya! Woo!

FIG. 5–1   Jack wrote and performed a song about a problem he saw in the classroom.

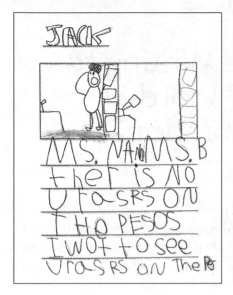
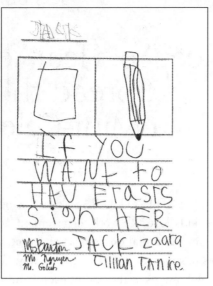

Ms. N and Ms. B,
There is no erasers on
the pencils. I want to
see erasers on there.
If you want to have
erasers, sign here.

FIG. 5–2   Jack's petition

his pieces and began to wave them in the air. "I just can't decide!" he wailed. "My marker song and my petition about erasers! I like them both." See CD-ROM for Jack's song.

"Jack, sometimes choosing a piece to publish can be very challenging, especially for a writer like you who has a folder full of spectacular writing. Now remember, the point of persuasive writing is to call others to action, to get other people to help you fix the problems that you are noticing. Is there one problem that is more important to you than the other?"

Jack looked down at the writing in his hands, back and forth from one to the other. "I really, really want to have some new pencils with erasers. And other kids do, too! See, look how many kids signed my petition! I think I'm going to publish my petition." I then convened the class, and did a quick symphony share, gesturing for writers who seemed to have a clear sense of direction to share their plans.

Hear Ye! Hear Ye! Writing to Spread the Word (a Mini-Celebration)

IN THIS SESSION, you'll teach students that opinion writers get their words out into the world to enable change.

GETTING READY

✔ Demonstration writing from Bend I (see Teaching and Active Engagement)

✔ "Writers Write to Make the World Better!" chart (see Teaching and Active Engagement)

✔ A piece of writing that each student has selected for publication prior to today's minilesson (see Teaching and Active Engagement)

✔ Opinion Writing Checklist, Grades K and 1 as a chart as well as individual copies for each student (see Mid-Workshop Teaching)

✔ A strip of star stickers for each student (see Mid-Workshop Teaching)

COMMON CORE STATE STANDARDS: W.K.1, W.K.5, W.K.6, W.1.1, RFS.K.1, RFS.K.2, RFS.K.3, SL.K.1, SL.K.3, SL.K.4, SL.K.5, SL.K.6, L.K.1, L.K.2, L.K.6

ENERGY AND ENTHUSIASM are driving forces for any successful unit of study. When kids love the work, engagement and volume will undoubtedly follow. To maintain the initial excitement of a unit, it often helps to give students multiple opportunities to share their work along the way. For this reason, we tend to conduct small publishing celebrations at the end of each bend rather than waiting until the end of the unit. This session gives students a chance to publish their opinion writing while reminding them of the underlying purpose of this new genre—building awareness of problems in the world and convincing people to help make a change. This mindfulness of audience drives writers, and supporting audience awareness is especially important when teaching young children, as the egocentricity of youngsters means that kindergartners are not apt to think about readers as being different from themselves. This initial bend has asked kindergartners to consider problems they've seen and experienced, then write in ways that help people understand, and ultimately, address these issues.

To set up for today's minilesson, you asked your students to look back across their pieces and choose one that they'd like to publish. During today's minilesson, you'll now ask writers to consider audience, deciding *who*, specifically, needs to hear these words, so they can then seek out the audience that can actually enable the change they envision to take place. With this clearer sense of audience, students will plan on the best way to publicize their work—perhaps posting signs or posters around the classroom or school, perhaps deciding to read their books to buddies in another class, perhaps delivering letters and cards to the recipients, perhaps forming a chorus and singing their songs as they parade in and out of other classrooms. Other writers might have envisioned a change that requires reaching a larger audience, and these writers might need to do an added piece of writing, perhaps writing to the school principal to ask if it is possible to make an announcement on the school loudspeaker or at recess on the bullhorn. In either case, the aim of this session is to build students' understanding of the purpose of persuasive writing by allowing them to reach readers. It is important that students are given a chance to send their words out into the world now, when the unit is still young, because they will write differently as they continue in this unit after having had this opportunity.

"To maintain the initial excitement of a unit, it often helps to give students multiple opportunities to share their work along the way."

Just before students send their work out into the world, challenge them to recall all they now know about persuasive writing, and with the aid of a checklist, to look back over their work and quickly fix up their piece just a bit more.

Although your minilesson will ask the class to make plans for ways they will share their writing with others, narrowing in on a target audience, you'll expect that kindergartners may make plans that require a little extra help and guidance. Some may need to make copies in the office, visit other classrooms to read letters or sing chants, and some may need to deliver their writing to specialists throughout the school. You might decide to ask for assistance from upper-grade buddies or parent volunteers so that you have people to chaperone your students in pairs or small groups.

You'll probably expect some students will not have a chance to share their work during today's writing workshop. Some of the publishing will thread through the upcoming day or two, as opportunities present themselves.

Hopefully there will be opportunities later for children to look forward, as well as looking backwards. The day should fill them with intentions and resolve for the upcoming bend in the unit.

Hear Ye! Hear Ye! Writing to Spread the Word (a Mini-Celebration)

CONNECTION

Tell of a time on TV when many people protested a problem. Suggest that those people resemble your students save one thing: they had an audience. Your students need one.

"Last night I was watching the news on television. The news story was covering a new parking garage that is being built on top of an old baseball field. The reporter was interviewing some people at the construction site. Many of them did not want the baseball field to be torn down. An older man said that the baseball field had been there for many years. He had a lot of happy memories playing there when he was much younger. A little boy even got in front of the camera and gave his opinion. He explained how upset he felt because he wouldn't be able to play baseball there anymore. He didn't think a parking garage should replace it. Then, he spoke right into the reporter's microphone and said, 'Please build the garage somewhere else, instead! We love playing baseball here.'

"As I was watching this story and listening to these people give their opinions on TV, I realized something. *You* are doing this in our writing workshop! You've been working on all kinds of writing to tell people about the opinions *you* have and the problems *you* see and the ways *you* want to make things better.

"Except there's one big difference. The people on TV were sharing their opinions with a *lot* of people. Everyone who watched the news heard about this problem. But the problems that you've been writing about are tucked away in your folders. We have to make sure we let people know about these problems, so they can help fix them!"

❧ **Name the teaching point.**

"Today I want to teach you that opinion writers don't wait around quietly, hoping that someone will ask to learn their opinion. Opinion writers get their words out into the world so lots of people will be able to know and care about the message."

◆ COACHING

Opinion writing is meant to be contextualized in the real world, so it makes sense that you'd tell stories of people picketing and petitioning to save a beloved baseball field, and old elm, or a stray kitten. When you tell stories like this you help children know that writing is worth doing and doing well. It saves lives!

Frank Smith writes, "Written language is for stories to be read, songs to be sung, newspapers to be shared, letters to be mailed, jokes to be told...."

TEACHING AND ACTIVE ENGAGEMENT

Channel children to watch as you demonstrate the process of rereading your text, thinking about who needs to read it.

"Today let's think about actually getting our writing out into the world so people can read it and so things get better. I'll start by making a plan for how to do that with our class writing about running in the hallways. You can watch what I do to think about getting this writing out into the world. Then, after our minilesson is over, when you go back to your writing spots, you'll have time to talk with your partner about what *you* can do to send your writing into the world.

"You ready to watch what I do so you and your partner can later do the same sort of work?"

I picked up the piece, "So first, let me decide *who* should read this. Who can actually help with my cause?" I motioned toward the chart, highlighting the fourth step.

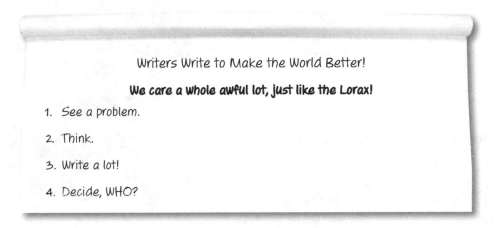

Writers Write to Make the World Better!

We care a whole awful lot, just like the Lorax!

1. See a problem.

2. Think.

3. Write a lot!

4. Decide, WHO?

"Hmm. Do I want to send it home to mothers and fathers? No! They don't run in our halls. Who does? Hmm. I think it is mostly *the kids* who need to read this—and especially the big kids who run and push. I'm going to write who this is for on a sticky note."

Channel children to ask the same question of the piece of writing they have selected to publish.

"So, writers, can you try to do the same thing I just did? Thumbs up if you remember what the question was that I was asking myself."

I left a little pool of silence, giving children time to answer that question for themselves if they could, and then said, "I know a lot of you are remembering that I asked, '*Who* needs to read this?'" I pointed to the fourth step of the chart as I restated the question. "Can you reread your own writing and think about that question for your writing? Do that quietly, without talking to anyone."

FIG. 6–1

Notice that this minilesson proceeds 'I do, you do, I do' and then children are sent off for the next 'you do.' That is, the active engagement section of the minilesson is here, inserted in between two demonstrations.

After a minute, I said, "How many of you are thinking that kids in this class need to read your writing—so that you might post it somewhere here in this room or read it at a class meeting?" A few thumbs went up. "How many of you are thinking that you may need to read your writing to a bunch of classes or to hang it somewhere around the school?" More thumbs went up. "Are there other places where your writing might need to go—like the cafeteria or the library or the schoolyard?" Again, some children signaled with thumbs up.

Channel writers to watch as you do one more step, thinking about how your writing can reach the readers it needs to reach. This time, demonstrate the work children will do back at their seats with their partners.

"Next, I better think about how I can get our writing to those readers. Do we hang it somewhere or mail it or carry it—or what?" I slowly flipped through the pages of the book about running in the halls, as if rereading to myself. Then I thought out loud, "Maybe we can read this book in every classroom, so everybody in the school knows about this problem and helps fix it.

"What could we do right *now* to make that happen?

"Well, I think we first need to read over our book and make sure it is finished, and then I need to write a letter to the teachers to ask if I can come to their class to read it. Then I have to ask Ms. Lotz in the front office if I can make copies of the letter and put it into every teacher's mailbox. Whew, that is *a lot* to do in one day, so I better get started!"

LINK

Send writers off to make plans (at their desks) with partners for what they need to do today to make sure their writing reaches readers.

"So, writers, I think you know that opinion writers don't just wait around, hoping that someone will ask to learn their opinion. Opinion writers get their words out into the world so lots of people will be able to know and care about stuff they care about. To do this, opinion writers need to decide, '*Who* needs to read this?' and 'How will I get my words to that reader, or those readers?'

"My plan for this piece is to read it over and make sure it is ready to be shared, then to write a letter to every teacher asking if she will read this book aloud, and to ask Ms. Lotz if she'll let me make copies. I have a lot to do. You still need to make plans. So right now, grab your writing and rush back to your writing spots, and will you and your partner reread each of your pieces of writing, and then talk about who needs to read those pieces of writing and what do you need to do today to make that happen? Go! Fast!"

Using Conferences to Assess and to Plan for Future Teaching

BECAUSE TODAY MARKS THE END OF THE FIRST BEND, you'll want to use this as an opportunity to take an inventory of your class, reflecting on the work they have done to decide on next steps, including deciding on the small-group work you'll address today and across the upcoming days. You might reflect on the following:

◆ Does the writing this child produce suggest that he or she can write differently when the purpose is to persuade rather than when telling a story, or teaching someone a topic?

◆ Does the child's persuasive writing show that the child can state an opinion and provide a reason or two?

◆ Can the child draw on information or knowledge about the world (i.e., the classroom, the school, the family) to support his or her opinion?

Additionally, you'll assess use of spelling and conventions, especially those outlined by the Common Core Language Standards.

◆ Are my students writing in full sentences?

◆ Leaving spaces between words?

◆ Using end punctuation?

◆ Using capitals?

◆ Representing most sounds in simple words?

Today you'll ask students to use the kindergarten and first-grade checklists to reflect on their writing and to make plans for ways to improve the piece prior to publishing. You'll probably notate your own mental checklist of students who require additional supports with structure, elaboration, spelling, or conventions.

Perhaps you will convene a group of students who provided just one reason to support their opinion. If you can play the devil's advocate and argue against their reason, you can force them to generate alternative reasons. This friendly debate can serve as rehearsal, just as oral storytelling does when children are writing narratives.

You may also convene a group of students who struggle with conventions. You might ask them to bring white boards and dry erase markers. You could, then, engage the group in an interactive writing session, making a point to embed work on conventions into a shared piece of writing.

Students need to be able to share their opinions, loud and proud, for all the world to hear. Finally, you might convene a small group of children who could profit from help reading their writing persuasively.

After the mid-workshop teaching point, your conferring and small-group work will support children in using the checklist to mobilize urgent revisions. You'll convene a small group of writers who are ready to tackle the Grade 1 checklist.

Before calling students back to the meeting area, I set a copy of the Opinion Writing Checklist and a strip of star stickers on each rug spot. "Writers," I called, "please join me in the meeting area with the writing that you are working on right now?" Once the students gathered, I continued. "I have something I want to share with you—another writing tool." I pointed to the enlarged Opinion Writing Checklist displayed in the meeting area and gestured toward the copies at their feet. "It is the checklist that you'll be using to set goals and reflect on the progress you are making as opinion writers. I know many of you remember doing this earlier in the year when you were writing true stories from your life and how-to books. This chart is a little bit different though, since these goals are all about opinion writing. In a moment, I'm going to read each item on the list. We're going to do the same thing with this checklist as we did with our true stories and how-to checklists. Get your star stickers ready! Remember what we did with those star stickers in our how-to books? As I read through the items on the checklist, you will use your stars to find places in your writing where you are do-

Opinion Writing Checklist

	Kindergarten	NOT YET	STARTING TO	YES!	Grade 1	NOT YET	STARTING TO	YES!
	Structure				**Structure**			
Overall	I told, drew, and wrote my opinion or likes and dislikes about a topic or book.	☐	☐	☐	I wrote my opinion or my likes and dislikes and said why.	☐	☐	☐
Lead	I wrote my opinion in the beginning.	☐	☐	☐	I wrote a beginning in which I got readers' attention. I named the topic or text I was writing about and gave my opinion.	☐	☐	☐
Transitions	I wrote my idea and then said more. I used words such as *because*.	☐	☐	☐	I said more about my opinion and used words such as *and* and *because*.	☐	☐	☐
Ending	I had a last part or page.	☐	☐	☐	I wrote an ending for my piece.	☐	☐	☐
Organization	I told my opinion in one place and in another place I said why.	☐	☐	☐	I wrote a part where I got readers' attention and a part where I said more.	☐	☐	☐
	Development				**Development**			
Elaboration	I put everything I thought about the topic (or book) on the page.	☐	☐	☐	I wrote at least one reason for my opinion.	☐	☐	☐
Craft	I had details in pictures and words.	☐	☐	☐	I used labels and words to give details.	☐	☐	☐
	Language Conventions				**Language Conventions**			
Spelling	I could read my writing.	☐	☐	☐	I used all I knew about words and chunks of words (*at, op, it,* etc.) to help me spell.	☐	☐	☐
	I wrote a letter for the sounds I heard.	☐	☐	☐	I spelled all the word wall words right and used the word wall to help me spell other words.	☐	☐	☐
	I used the word wall to help me spell.	☐	☐	☐				

ing those things really well. You can put a star right there in your writing! And do you remember what you do if you can't find a place in your writing where you are doing something from the checklist? You shoot for the stars! You will put your star on the checklist, if this is something you are still doing halfway or not at all, something that will become a goal for you. There is nothing more exciting than finding goals! So let's try it. As I read through each item on the checklist, put a star on your writing if you are already doing this. And if not, put a star on the checklist. You ready?" I read through each bullet on the kindergarten checklist, giving students a chance to look over their opinion writing and place stars accordingly. The Opinion Writing Checklist, Grades K and 1 can be found on the CD-ROM.

"Writers, as we were going through the checklist, I saw lots of stars flying! Some going into your writing, but also many are going right onto your checklist. And you know what? Stars on your checklist are great. Because now, you know *exactly* what else you need to do to get your piece ready for publishing! You have some more time to work on your writing, and you probably know just what you need to do!"

Speaking Out, Loud and Proud

Show the students how your tone of voice and volume influences the attention others pay to you. Speak in a quiet timid voice and then for contrast, speak out, loud and proud.

Once all the students were gathered in the meeting area with their soon to be published pieces, I began speaking, in a meek, timid voice, barely audible above the transition chatter. "Um, excuse me. Writers? Writers, can I have your eyes up here? Please?" A few students looked up at me with a puzzled expression, but many continued chatting with a neighbor or looking over their writing. I continued on, in my quiet voice. "Writers? Please. I have something I want to say. Why won't anyone listen to me?" I still did not have the attention of many in the class.

I shifted gears, now speaking in a voice that was loud and proud, projecting to the group. "Writers, eyes up here please. I have something very important to share with you!" The chatter stopped. I had everyone's attention.

"You know, it took a long time to get everyone to listen to me when you first came to the rug. Any ideas why that was?"

"I couldn't even hear you!" said Shane.

"Yeah," Kimani added. "You were so quiet! Like a mouse!"

"And why were you talking like that?" asked Shane. "You were talking like you were shy."

Explain that the way a person talks influences the way others perceive the message. Give students an opportunity to practice reading their writing in persuasive fashion.

"Writers, you are right! The way I was talking made it feel like no one *should* pay attention to what I have to say. I wasn't talking in a way that said 'listen up.'

"Today you've begun celebrating your writing. For those of you who haven't shared your writing, I want to remind you that you need to speak in a way that makes people know the hopes we have for the world. To do that, it helps to practice reading your writing in a way that shows your audience just how important those words are! When I talked to you in that *teeny tiny* little voice, no one listened! But when I spoke in that big proud, loud voice, everyone paid attention!"

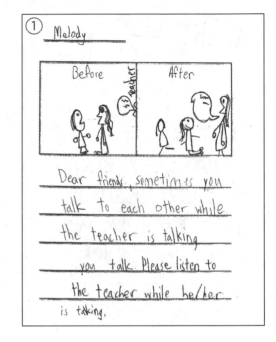

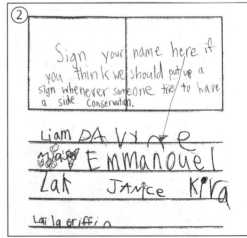

FIG. 6–2 Melody's petition

"Let's get together with friends right now and share writing in small groups. Take turns reading your pieces out loud, practicing your best reading voice. Make it smooth, and be sure to show the big feelings you have about your topic. Remember, you are trying to make change happen! Talk in a way that will get people to really listen!"

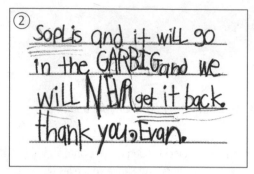

Dear K-126, Please try to keep your supplies on the table or else we will not have a lot of supplies and it will go in the GARBAGE and we will NEVER get it back. Thank you, Evan

FIG. 6–3   Evan's letter

Do not drop markers

FIG. 6–4   Jonathan's sign

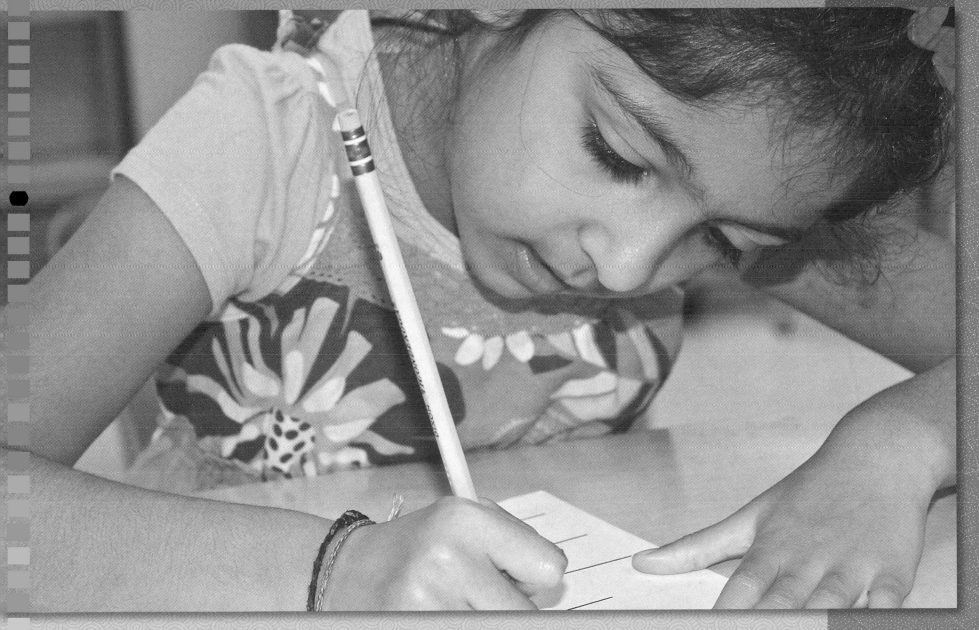

Sending Our Words Out Into the World: Writing Letters to Make a Change

BEND II

Writing Letters that Reach Readers

IN THIS SESSION, you'll teach students that writers write letters as if they are talking to their reader.

GETTING READY

✔ "Writers Write to Make the World Better!" chart (see Connection)

✔ *Click, Clack, Moo: Cows that Type* by Doreen Cronin (see Connection)

✔ Chart paper and marker (see Teaching and Link)

✔ A variety of letter-writing paper choices (see Link)

COMMON CORE STATE STANDARDS: W.K.1, W.1.1, RL.K.1, RFS.K.1, RFS.K.2, RFS.K.3, SL.K.1, SL.K.4, SL.K.5, SL.K.6, L.K.1, L.K.2, L.K.6

T HIS SESSION MARKS THE START OF A NEW BEND. Your students have been working feverishly on writing that bears considerable weight and significance. Granted, sometimes it is a stretch to characterize the writing done by five- and six-year-olds as having weight and significance. After all, Johnny's sign requesting candy instead of green beans for lunch doesn't immediately strike one as having great significance. But then again, it is not a small deal that the youngsters in your care are coming to realize that they can use writing to make stuff happen. For now, the changes they seek may be ridding lunchtime of vegetables, but soon, writers like Johnny will discover that opinion writing can make the world better not just for themselves but for others, too. And *that* understanding is a powerful one.

You've not only taught your writers to look around and see possibilities for all the ways words can make the world a better place. You've also helped them to see genre as flexible and to reach for a specific genre to accomplish particular purposes. In the last week or two, children have been immersed in a whole range of kinds of writing: signs, petitions, songs, letters, cards, books, lists.

Starting today, this unit will become more traditional. Your instruction will help children become familiar with one particular genre, learning to do that kind of writing well. The genre you'll teach for this upcoming bend is that of persuasive letters.

You may hesitate to move so quickly from the wide-open terrain of the first bend toward this one kind of writing, and of course you can prolong Bend I if you choose. We decided to hone in on persuasive letters because we believe this can provide a forum for teaching the qualities and processes of strong persuasive writing. So in that spirit, onward we go!

As you journey through this second bend, you'll encourage your children to move away from personal problems towards more shared problems. Among other things, they'll write about the ways the school and the neighborhood could be better, crafting letters that help fix problems in the community.

During today's session, you will, first, rally children to join in on a whole-class cause by writing letters that help redesign and equip the classroom writing center so that it resembles a post office, with baskets of envelopes and return address labels beside paper choice trays. You'll coach writers to imagine that their reader is standing beside them and to

---

"You've taught your writers to see possibilities for ways words can make the world a better place, but also to see genre as flexible and to reach for a specific genre to accomplish particular purposes."

think about what they need to tell that person, talking right to the reader, before writing those words in their letters. This way, you'll help students write in a voice that speaks to the reader. Before you send children off to write, you will display an example of a letter that will help kids quickly orient themselves to the conventions of the new genre so they record the date in the corner and the greeting in the appropriate place.

Before you launch this bend, it will be helpful if you can spend some time during your read-alouds immersing your students in books that help them get a feel for letter writing. For instance, you might choose from picture books such as *I Wanna New Room* by Karen Kaufman Orloff, *Click, Clack, Moo: Cows that Type* by Doreen Cronin, or *Corduroy Writes a Letter* by Alison Inches. Each of these examples not only exposes your kindergartners to the format and audience of a letter, but also illustrates how writers can use a persuasive letter as a means to achieve their goals, to get their point across. Ask—in the form of a persuasive letter—and ye shall receive!

As always, this work will be done on a variety of paper, each version offers different amounts of support. Some of your children will benefit from paper that provides the support of picture boxes that channel writers to sketch the problem they see and the change they seek. You will have given others paper that channels them to get right to their words.

Writing Letters that Reach Readers

CONNECTION

Share examples of the writing that children sent into the world during the last session already yielding some effects.

"Writers, come right away, find your rug spots, and let's get started because we have so much to talk about." I waited until the children were with me, hustling them quickly into place to create a nice sense of energy. "Writers, your writing was working its magic this morning. Some of you were starting to heave your coats into our coat closet, and then I actually saw you take in Will's sign and change your actions. And look!" I threw open the doors to the coat room. "Will's writing did that—amazing. The power of the pen." (See Figure 7–1.)

> Do not throw your coats! Hang up your backpack. You will make a big mess and you won't find anything!

Orient children to the upcoming bend by saying that whereas before they wrote many kinds of writing to make a difference in the world, for the next week or two, they'll focus on letter writing.

"So far in this unit, you've been working on all kinds of writing—making lists and songs and signs and petitions—to help make the classroom and our whole school better. I'm thinking that for you to learn to get really, really good at writing in ways that make kids take care of the coat closet and that get our principal supplying us with more books, we should spend the next week or two learning to write one kind of writing really well. I know you love the story *Click, Clack, Moo: Cows that Type* as much as I do. Remember how those cows wrote letters to Farmer Brown to tell him the barn was too cold and to convince him to bring them electric blankets? Those cows wrote letters to recruit Farmer Brown to help, and I am thinking we could learn to write that sort of letter really well, spending a few weeks just working on writing powerful letters. Are you game for that?" The children signaled that they were.

Refer to the "Writers Write to Make the World Better" anchor chart to review how writers go about writing something that makes a difference, showing that letter writing is a subset of what they have been doing. Follow the chart to generate the content and audience for your letter.

"Before we can write letters, we need to remember how writers go about writing to make things better in the world. Remember that earlier, we said that writers do a bunch of things."

FIG. 7–1 Will's sign calls classmates to action, including reasons and consequnces.

"Let's do those things." I pointed to each item as I proceeded through the list. "We need to think about a problem. Before, we mostly thought about problems that we saw in our classroom or school. But now, I'd like us to also think about the problems we see, the things we want to fix, *outside* of school. What are you noticing in the community or even at home? Hmm. For my writing I'm remembering how so many kids complain all the time about stuff that happens at the park down the street. I see it, too, when I am walking by there on my way home! Kids don't wait their turn in line for the slide, older kids play a little rough, kids throw balls and don't pay attention to who is around them. Maybe, if you help me, we could write a letter it will help us fix that problem."

"Yeah, but who will that letter be for?" asked Tom.

"The grown-ups at the playground!" Jaden added. "You know, the babysitters and moms and dads and grandmas and stuff!"

I nodded. "So Jaden, you just jumped ahead to our next steps. You are suggesting that a way to fix this is to ask the grown-ups to talk to kids about it?"

The kids all nodded vigorously. "Let's get started on that, then."

❖ Name the teaching point.

"I want you give you one tip to help you write *powerful* letters. When you are writing a letter, it helps to imagine the person is standing right beside you, and then you almost talk to the person, only you are talking to the page."

TEACHING

Demonstrate the thin line between talking to someone and writing to that person. Start the letter the class has decided to write by saying sentences to imaginary readers, sitting near, and then recording what you say.

"So let's work on a letter together, and let's pretend the grown-ups we see at the park are right here next to us." I turned my body as if to address these imaginary grown-ups directly, but then, in an aside, spoke to remind children of our goal. "We want to ask them to help children play nicer at the park. And remember, first we will tell them about the problem and give details or examples."

Returning to the imaginary guests, I said, "So. 'Hi Moms, Dads, Babysitters, and Grandmas.' Umm . . . "

In an aside to the children, I mentioned, "They're probably thinking, 'What's going on, right? I better explain why we wanted to talk to them. Um, what do we say?"

I recall the first time I was interviewed on the radio. The person audiotaping told me that instead of imagining that I was sending my language out on the airwaves to people across the world, I'd do better to act as if the microphone was another person, sitting right beside me, and to talk intimately, informally, to the mike.

I left a little space for children to begin thinking about possible messages. Then I started talking, using words that would become my letter.

April 2

Moms, Dads, Babysitters, and Grandmas,

Can we talk to you about a problem that my kids and I are seeing? Some kids at the park are not playing nicely. Can you help us fix this problem? Kids aren't waiting patiently in line for the slide. And sometimes bigger kids play too rough. Like, for example . . . um . . .

I quickly recorded the beginning of the letter. I included several letter-writing conventions, such as the greeting and date, but didn't make a big deal about them. I then turned back to the class, recruiting their help. I asked, "Is there a true story that we could tell about a time when we saw this problem happen? Do you have an example that won't hurt anyone's feelings?"

Jonathan said, "One time there was this big kid, and he was running so fast down the ramp that he knocked over a little kid who was trying to walk up it! He bumped right into him and knocked him down. He didn't even stop!"

"He should've helped the little kid get up and make sure he was okay," Zaara added.

I nodded and continued with the letter:

April 2

Dear Moms, Dads, Babysitters, and Grandmas,

Can we talk to you about a problem that my kids and I are seeing? Some kids at the park are not playing nicely. Can you help us fix this problem? Kids aren't waiting patiently in line for the slide. And sometimes bigger kids play too rough. One time, a big kid went running so fast down the ramp that he knocked a little kid over. And the big kid didn't even stop, to see if the little kid was okay, and help him up.

I turned to the invisible grown-ups beside me and asked, "Are you noticing that, too?" Then I said, "Oh, I better add that, too," and wrote that down in the letter.

Are you noticing that this is a problem, too?

This minilesson has an extremely long link, as you end up channeling the class into some coordinated shared work. The net result of that is that we are keeping this portion as streamlined as possible.

This is an extremely long text to produce within a minilesson. Write quickly!

ACTIVE ENGAGEMENT

After writing half the letter yourself, with input, pass the baton to children. Ask them to write-in-the-air what they would write. Then tap the class for some content to add to the letter.

I added, "They probably want us to give some reasons that this is a problem. Can Partner One pretend to be one of the grown-ups at the park and Partner Two, tell your reasons for thinking it is a problem that kids not playing nicely. Turn and talk."

Davin immediately said to his partner, "Because the park should be fun for everyone!"

Meanwhile Shane said to his partner, "Kids gotta play nice or people get hurt."

After a minute or two more, I reconvened the class and took a few suggestions from the group. Then I said, "Now watch," and added the following.

> Are you noticing that this is a problem, too? We want to fix this because the park should be a fun place for everyone. We don't want anyone to get hurt.

I turned back to the group. "Impressive letter, friends! We can write an 'or else…' part and work on ideas for how to fix the problem in the park later."

LINK

Retell the work you did today, reiterating the teaching point, doing all this in ways that are transferable to another day and another text.

"So, writers, just like the cows wrote to Farmer Brown, you can send letters to people who might help fix problems you see. I am hoping that you got the idea that writers write letters that," and I referenced the chart, "aim to fix a problem in the world. And I hope you learned that to do this, it can help for the writer to pretend the reader is right there and talk to the reader. The writer often tells the reader the problem and the reasons why that is a problem, adding in some details."

Suggest that instead of children dispersing to each work on an individual letter—the topics of which still need to be generated—they instead each write someone to support developing a post office for the class.

"Today I have an idea for a change that I think really needs to happen, and I wonder if you would *all* be willing to write letters to help make that change come true. I think we need fancy letter-writing paper in our classroom so when we write our letters, they can be on special paper."

"Yeah, and envelopes!" Gabriella offered.

Remember that once you have learned from a few individuals, it's best to move units along. That way you save time for children to write.

You'll be writing on chart paper in front of the class, which is a slow process, so we encourage you to keep your text brief. Tell children about the portions of it you can write later.

"Stamps, too!" Diego added.

"You are giving me a new idea. What if we tried to write letters to convince people to help us set up a whole post office in our classroom?"

"I can write to my dad. He's a mailman! I'm gonna ask him for those sticky labels," Jeffrey called out.

"Who else has ideas for who you could write?" I said. "Turn and talk."

Mobilize the class to write letters to support a class post office today. Lower your standards so the letters actually get written in one day. You have the whole bend for learning to do this well. Now is the time for hasty approximations.

"We need to write *fast* if we are going to get supplies starting tomorrow, so let's first think up a list of who we could write. Every one of you needs to write a letter today to help with our project. So let's come up with some ideas. Who can you write? Who can help?"

Soon the children had made this list, which I jotted on chart paper.

the principal	money for stamps
parents	can kids deliver mail to the school
big brothers/sisters	writing paper and envelopes from home
parents	addresses
other teachers	do they want to do this too?

I voiced over to the class, "Decide who you will be writing, and then ask your partner to pretend to be that person. Say out loud the words you are going to write. When you are sure who you are writing and what you want to say, get started—fast! I have our letter up here on the easel to help you remember how letters go on the page." I pointed to the date, the salutation, and so forth. Of course, the model letter (Figure 7–2) supports more than just letter-writing conventions.

April 2

Dear Moms, Dads, Babysitters, and Grandmas,

Can we talk to you about a problem that my kids and I are seeing? Some kids at the park are not playing nicely. Can you help us fix this problem? Kids aren't waiting patiently in line for the slide. And sometimes bigger kids play too rough. One time, a big kid went running so fast down the ramp that he knocked a little kid over. And the big kid didn't even stop, to see if the little kid was okay, and help him up. Are you noticing that this is a problem, too? We want to fix this because the park should be a fun place for everyone. We don't want anyone to get hurt.

From,

Class K-139

FIG. 7–2   You may want to post this letter beside the other post office supplies. This will serve as an exemplar across the unit,

Small-Group Work to Support the Causes and Conventions of Letter Writing

TODAY YOUR GOAL WILL BE to help as many kids as possible write letters that encompass the structure and voice of the genre, selecting an audience and directing their words toward a specific recipient. You'll also want to help children draw on all they know about persuasive writing to write letters in which the writer states his or her opinion and supports it with reasons, perhaps embellishing them with details.

Because students have rallied around a class cause, group work will be especially efficient. If some children seem to falter, confused by the new paper or by the proposal to compose a letter, you will probably want to cluster those children together and help them all to envision how this work can roll out. In small groups, you can remind children that the work they will be doing today is not very different from the work they did during the first bend in this unit when they were making signs and songs and petitions and books to address problems they saw in the classroom. You might say, "Just like when you wrote petitions or songs, or made signs to tell people about the problems in our class and our school and all the reasons why these problems needed to be fixed, in your letter you'll tell your reader about the problem you see and all the reasons why it is a problem that needs fixing. It's the same! The big difference is when you are writing a letter, you know from the start who you are writing, and it is almost as if you're talking right to that person."

Don't underestimate the importance of teaching the conventions of letter writing. You could shrug this off, thinking, "It is not all that important that kindergartners use correct salutations," and that is true, but on the other hand it is terribly important that young children role-play their way into using a genre for real purposes, and taking on the conventions of letter writing helps a writer position himself or herself. Some writers will pick up on the format of a letter quickly. This is a good opportunity to allow writers to do some analysis and problem solving on their own, asking them to study finished letters and to decide what is required.

If you want to help writers plan their letters before jumping right to recording words, you might provide letter paper that includes picture boxes, and coach some children to sketch their plan, communicating key points in each picture box. Coach in, "What do you want to tell your reader first? Sketch that!" Then "Why is that so important?" Then "What's another reason why?" Or "What might happen if they don't help?" These drawings will serve as a scaffold for the sentences students will later add to their letters.

(continues)

MID-WORKSHOP TEACHING   Draw on All You Already Know

Standing in the middle of the hubbub, I spoke in a loud voice to get children's attention, and then waited. "Writers," I said. "It's important to remember everything you already know about convincing people. When you made signs and wrote songs and lists and petitions, you made sure to include *lots* of reasons, even telling the reader what might happen if they don't help! You wrote, 'We need to do this *or else.…*' You can do this when you write letters, too.

"Right now, think about all the reasons the class needs a post office. Have you added those? Have you added an 'or else'? What will happen if we don't get the supplies we need for writing letters? Make your letter as convincing as possible."

As Students Continue Working . . .

Speaking above the bustle of the room, I said, "You can staple on more pages or tape on revision strips if you need more space to write all of these ideas!" I gestured toward the writing center to encourage the students to write with increased volume.

Meanwhile, you will also want to help your most proficient writers plan their writing. Some teachers coach these writers to touch the lines while rehearsing their sentences aloud, in this way planning how their letter will go across each page. You'll probably interject lean, coaching prompts, similar to those you gave writers who were sketching across pages. "I'm writing to tell you . . . " Then, pushing her to elaborate, "Because . . . " Then "Another reason is . . . " Or "What might happen if they don't help?" Then echo back their letter in its entirety, as you touch the lines down the page, to help writers transfer their oral plan to writing.

FIG. 7–3   Hubert's letter

Dear Dad,
Can you buy some things for our post office and give us mail stamps and mail things.

Writing to Equip a Class Post Office

Provide some closure on the post office letter project and set writers up to expect that by tomorrow, they'll need to be ready to write letters on topics of their own choosing.

"Writers, most of you finished your letters today. Give them to me, and during lunch I'll try to get them sent out. I know a few of you are making your letter pages long so you will want a little more time to work on these tomorrow, and that is okay too. We should be able to gather what we need to get our post office up and running. Look, Zaara wrote a letter to Mr. G asking for stamps (see Figure 7–4). And Evan wrote a letter to Ms. Lotz (see Figure 7–5 on the following page), asking for envelopes. Another very important item for a working post office!"

"Even if your post office letter is not totally done, tomorrow you will start another letter, this time on a project, a cause, or an issue that you care about. I know that like me, you are probably finding that you walk through your days getting more and more ideas for ways things could get better and for the writing you could do. I wish we could take a walk right now through the school and the neighborhood and your homes, with clipboards in hand, jotting down all the ideas for things that could be better, for writing we could do."

Provide guided practice to coach children to imagine letting everything they see and do in a day spark ideas for letters. Help kids generate topics for tomorrow's letter writing.

"For now, let's pretend we are *all* walking through the neighborhood, and as we walk, we are looking around and thinking, 'What's not perfect here? What could be better?'

"Now you're walking into the playground. Think about what you usually do at the playground, and about how things are going, not just for you but for other people, too. In your imagination, look around and see what you see. What problems do you see that could be better? What might make things better?" I left a pool of silence. "Turn and tell your partner what you are thinking.

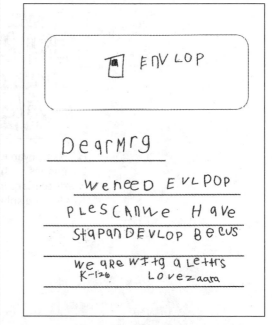

FIG. 7–4   Zaara is growing more aware of audience, directly addressing a teacher in her letter and using a friendly and polite tone to voice her request.

"Now it is time to go home. You are traveling home. What could be better? Turn and talk."

"Now you are in your house. You are playing in your own space. Or maybe you are helping out with chores. What could be better? Turn and talk."

Like kernels in a hot kettle, ideas popped quickly across the group. "Writers, make sure to remember these ideas because tomorrow you'll have a chance to write those letters."

FIG. 7–5   Evan is exploring and applying craft techniques, such as capitalized and underlined words to make important parts stand out. This letter displays his approximations.

Studying a Mentor Text
(a Guided Inquiry)

TODAY'S MINILESSON is designed not as explicit instruction, in which you demonstrate and then provide opportunities for scaffolded practice, but instead as an inquiry lesson, following the now-familiar template for this sort of teaching. This will be far from the first time your children have been invited to participate in a class investigation of a mentor text, aimed at extracting the replicable qualities of the text. This time, the goal is for children to work together to find the qualities that make the piece of writing persuasive.

As you have seen in previous lessons, the invitation to study a text, engaging in close reading of it, will yield surprising insights. Children see more than we might imagine possible. Even the youngest of writers grasp that some books (and in this case, some letters) beg to be read again and again, while others become forgotten on the shelf. The work of today's session is to identify, "Why?"

Children can pinpoint parts of a text—in this case a persuasive letter—that stand out for them, identifying words and lines and sections that give them strong feelings or reactions. Because they will be examining persuasive writing, you'll channel them to notice parts that especially convince them to want to help. Then you will ask children to try to figure out and to name what the author has done that makes those parts so effective.

Granted, your kindergartners probably won't be very proficient at talking about rhetorical moves. Your role in today's inquiry lesson is to listen closely to the observations they do make, echoing these observations back in ways that make the writer's process clear and replicable. That is to say, you'll help children name the techniques they admire and, ultimately, you'll co-construct a list of strategies for making letters more convincing.

You will probably want to introduce the letter that you study first as a read-aloud, so that children have time to talk first about its message. It is usually easiest to analyze how an author accomplishes his or her goals if one has first read the text as it was written to be read—for its content, not its craft. All that they learn from the shared inquiry into this mentor letter will be useful to them as children progress from editing their first letter (about the post office) to starting new letters. It is far easier to write well when a writer

IN THIS SESSION, you'll teach students that writers read and study the work of other writers and then try to incorporate what they have learned into their own writing.

GETTING READY

✔ Enlarged copy of Lily's letter as well as individual copies on clipboards for students (see Teaching and Active Engagement and Guided Inquiry) 🐾

✔ Star sticky notes or other Post-its (see Guided Inquiry)

✔ Chart paper and marker to list strategies for persuasive writing learned from mentor (see Guided Inquiry)

✔ "What Makes Writing Easy to Read" chart from the *Writing for Readers* unit (see Share)

COMMON CORE STATE STANDARDS: W.K.1, W.1.1, W.K.5, RI.K.1, RI.K.8, RI.K.10, SL.K.1, SL.K.3, SL.K.4, SL.K.5, L.K.1, L.K.2

has an image of good work to aim toward, and your students will have that image. You'll encourage them to use all they learn from studying the mentor text to aspire to write in ways that are convincing, right from the start. Your hope is that

---

"Your role in today's inquiry lesson is to listen closely to the observations students do make, echoing these observations back in ways that make the writer's process clear and replicable."

they don't just think about the content they want to put into a letter, but that they might also think, "How do I make this letter be a good one?"

Although your lesson will be aimed to support the new letters students will be writing and some fundamental concepts about letter writing, the whole class will not be working in sync because some students will continue to work on the letters they began yesterday when you galvanized the whole class to write in support of a class post office. That work also provides you with wonderful teaching opportunities because it is important for children to learn that writers recall all they know about making their writing easy to read before sending writing into the world. Audience is especially tangible when writing letters, so you may want to coach children to reread their letters as if they were the recipient and then work to clear up parts that don't sound quite right. Partners can provide new eyes, helping each other find ways to fix up letters before mailing them to their readers. Expect this work to manifest in different ways across your classroom. Some of your more novice writers may look back at a hard-to-decipher drawing and say, "Wait! Maybe he won't know what this is. I better put a label right here." Others may add finger spaces to separate squished-up words. More experienced writers may reread and decide, "This is confusing. I'm going to write this sentence again, so she gets what I mean."

In many ways, then, today's session will help students draft letters that are stronger and stronger—writing pieces that are more focused, more convincing, and easier to read—as they work across this second bend.

Studying a Mentor Text (a Guided Inquiry)

CONNECTION

Tell children that you set out to revise the shared letter you and the class had begun and realized you are not sure what makes for great persuasive writing.

Before students gathered in the meeting area for today's workshop, I set out copies of the mentor text, on clipboards, and pens for each student. "Writers, last night I sat down to work on the letter we worked on together about the playground problem. I wanted to make it the best letter in the world! I mean, if I want to fix this problem, the letter has to be really great.

"So, I sat down at my kitchen table, and I took out my revision pen, and I started wondering, 'What should I do to make *this* letter as good as it can be? And I realized that when we want to make *a story* as good as it can be, we look at a published story that we love and think, 'What works especially well in this story?' And we ask, 'What did the author do that I could do as well?' So to make a letter that is as good as it can be, it probably will help to look at a letter that people think is especially terrific and to ask, "What works especially well in this letter*?*" and "What did the letter writer do that I could do as well?"

Share a mentor text—a well-written persuasive letter, written by a child.

"The exciting news is that I have been given a copy of a letter that a child just a little older than you age wrote to her principal—and do you know what? The principal saved that little girl's letter for years and years in a special drawer of her desk. The fact that she saved that letter is a good sign that she thought it was a special one, so let's study it and see if we can learn how to write letters that are so special someone might save *our* letters.

"Listen up. Here is Lily's letter. There is a copy for each of you on the clipboard you are sitting near."

◆ COACHING

This lesson could just as easily be given to graduate students. It is infinitely interesting to analyze what the characteristics of good writing are across a range of genres. Consider, for a moment, how you would answer the question you are posing for your youngsters. The fact that the question would be intellectually interesting for you—and you are asking it to six-year-olds—is a clue that the DOK level of your teaching is high!

TEACHING AND ACTIVE ENGAGEMENT

Name a question that will guide the class inquiry. In this case, "What does Lily do to convince her reader to help her make things better?"

"This means that today I am not teaching you something. I am the same as you—a problem solver. Like you, I want to investigate, like detectives or scientists investigate, to find an answer to the question, 'What does Lily do in her letter that makes it a special one? What makes it a convincing letter?' And then we'll be able to ask, 'How can we do this in our letters, too?'"

GUIDED INQUIRY

Set writers up to investigate Lily's letter by guiding them through a series of steps that help students discover answers to the larger, overarching question. Then listen in and coach, eliciting and collecting comments.

"Okay, writers, the first thing we'll need to do is to find places in Lily's letter that we think are well-written. Right now, I am going to reread her letter. Will you find a part in it that seems especially well-written. When you hear a part that stands out for you, put a big star sticky note right next to that part." I reread the letter line by line, while students held on to their own copies, sticky notes in hand (see Figure 8–1).

> Dear Melanie,
>
> Did you know that kids are being too noisy on the stairs? It is a big problem. Some kids talk with inside voices. Other kids talk really loud. It's a problem because one day Felix was right next to me and he was yelling very loud and when Miss Liz said a quiet signal I could not hear her and I was not looking at her. It is bad. Maybe we can remind the kids to not yell by putting a sign on the wall on every staircase. It would be good for a lot of the 1st grade classes so when the teachers do a quiet signal they can hear the teacher so they can talk. Thank you, From Lily.

"Now, writers, here comes the really important part. You're going to ask yourselves a huge question. You're going to ask yourself *why* do you think the starred part is especially well-written? Look closely at it. Read it again and think, 'What did Lily do right here that stands out?' Do that quietly, by yourself, so you come up with your own idea about what Lily does in her writing."

Coach into children's work, prompting them to study Lily's structure, voice, word choice, and craft.

As children worked, I voiced over, "The answers don't usually just pop out, so listen to the part once more and ask yourself, 'What is it about the part I like that made me star it?' Think about the particular words she decided to use. Think about what she could have written, instead, and why she made the choices she did."

① Dear Melnie,

did you know that kids are being too noisey on the stairs it is a big problem. Some kids talk with inside voises. Ather kids talk relly loud. Its a problem because one day Felix was right next to me and he was yelling very loud and when Miss Liz said a quiet signel I could not hear her and I was

② not looking at her. It is bad. Maybe we can remind the kids to not yell bi putting a sighn on the wall on evry stair case. It would be good for a lot of the ~~clas~~ 1st grade classes so when the teachers do a quiet cignal they can hear the teacher so they can talk. thank you,

From
Lily

FIG. 8–1 Lily's letter

After I read through the letter once more, I said, "Writers, put a thumb up if you noticed one thing that Lily did that made her letter seem well-written, or that you think made it so that the principal saved the letters all these years." Thumbs shot up across the rug. Some children held up their letters, exposing stars marking key parts across the page.

"Writers, before you tell each other your thoughts, think about them again, and this time, make your thoughts more detailed. Point to a place on the page where the writer does what you notice. Think about what *exactly* makes that part stand out." After a moment, I said, "Turn and tell your partner what you notice."

Listen in and highlight observations that students make. Repeat their observations using more precise language, and record these on a chart.

I listened to one partnership. "Right over here, she used a good word—*because. Because* is a reason word," Rosa noted, pointing to a place in the letter that used the word *because*.

Her partner said nothing, so I asked, "And did Lily go from saying 'because . . . ' to giving a reason why it is a problem that people are so loud?"

Rosa responded by reading aloud a part of the letter. "One day Felix was right next to me and he was yelling very loud."

I spoke over the hubbub of partnership conversations. "Class, Rosa is pointing out that Lily did not just *say* that the stairs need to be quieter so people can hear. She also gave an example."

I moved on to hear Shane suggest that she gave fix-up ideas in her letter. "I bet that will help the principal know what to do to help fix the problem," I said.

Reconvene the group and restate the details students noticed to create a class list.

"Writers, I'm hearing you share so many great things Lily did to convince her reader. Let's make a big list of all of the things you noticed, so we can try to do those things in our letters, too." As kids made suggestions, I reworded them in ways that would be more universally applicable.

"She told the principal about the kids being too noisy," Lindsay offered.

"Everyone, point to a place in the text where Lily has named the problem, that the kids are noisy."

"Right here! At the beginning," Lindsay replied, holding up her copy of the letter.

"So, right at the beginning, Lily told her opinion. She thinks the kids being noisy is a big problem. Let's add that to our list." I charted this quickly. "What else?"

"She told a story," Rosa added.

The Common Core places a high priority on children learning to cite text-based evidence. This is a habit that children can begin developing at a very young age. It helps, of course, to give them copies of the text and to plan to reread the text many times.

I'd listened to children talking, so called on youngsters whose ideas would help the class and recorded the ideas on a chart.

Notice that I ask for specific text references. I rallied all the children to look for text evidence as a way to accentuate the process of doing this, and as a way, also, to keep kids active and involved.

"That's right, Rosa. She told a little story about a time she had this problem. That makes her letter really convincing." I added this to the list.

"And she put reasons," Jacob began, listing examples across his fingers, "like the kids talk really loud and she could not hear the teacher and it is bad."

"And she said, 'because.' That's a reason word," Rosa reiterated.

"Yes, you're right, Rosa. *Because* is a smart word to use when you want to give a reason. But it seems like Lily didn't just give the principal *one* reason why this is a problem. She gave *lots* of reasons. We should definitely add that to our list!"

"And the fix-it idea, too! With the signs," Shane reminded me.

"Did anyone notice the way Lily ended her letter to the principal? Look back and find that part on your copy." I waited for the children to turn to the closing.

"Oh! She said, 'Thank you, From Lily,'" Serena realized. "That's using manners."

"She *is* using manners, Serena. Maybe that's something else we can do to be really convincing. When you use polite words like *thank you*, it helps convince your reader to want to help. Should we add this to our list, too?" I asked. The class quickly agreed.

LINK

Set writers up to try one of these techniques on their own writing.

"Writers, this is a nice long list! I'm starting to see what makes Lily's letter so wonderful. I don't know about you, but I feel as if we could put some of these things in our letter. Do any of you feel that way, too?

"You're the ones who just made this whole list. So would you be willing to figure out how to use Lily's ideas to make your letters really great? You could go back to a letter you started yesterday and find ways to make that letter even better, or you could start a whole new letter today. I bet you already have ideas for ways to make it really great, right from the start!"

Send writers off to work independently.

"I want to just remind you that you can do this always! You can find writing you love and look for parts you think are simply the best. Then you can ask, 'What makes this so great?' to find ways to try it in your own writing. We can learn from all kinds of authors this way, to help us write in ways that are just as great as the writing they do."

Conferring to Help Students Use Mentor Texts for Revision Ideas

I N TODAY'S GUIDED INQUIRY LESSON you set students up to explore a mentor author, giving them a scaffolded opportunity to scour the text, looking for important crafting techniques. Some of your students will be brimming with excitement to "write like Lily." Others may need a bit more support from you.

Liam had written a letter to his big brother already, asking if he would try to listen better to Liam's writing. Now Liam felt sure he was done. I sympathized with him over his trouble with his big brother, and then said, "What we learned from Lily is that when she wanted to be heard, she did a lot of things in her writing so that people would hear her. Can you reread the list of all the things she did and tell me which of those things you are going to try as well?" Liam decided he wanted to add a "fix-up strategy" to his letter—a proposed solution. So he reread the letter, thinking about where he could add something (see Figure 8–2), and announced that he had no space.

I nudged Liam to solve his own problem. "So, what can you do when you need more space to write?"

He glanced over at the writing center. "Get more paper?" he tested.

"Whenever you think you'll need a *lot* more space, you can staple on another page. But if you need just a few more lines, you can tape on revision strips," I said. He decided to add a second page to his letter.

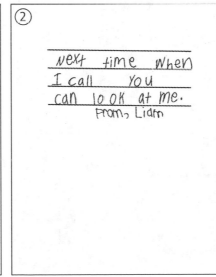

FIG. 8–2   Liam's letter to Ronen

Making Sure Writing Is Easy to Read

Remind kids that when they finish a letter, they need to make sure it is easy to read. Reference the chart from the earlier unit, asking writers to use it as a checklist.

"You have written a bunch of letters already, and we'll need to mail those letters out into the world. After all, if you want people to help make things better, you need to tell them your ideas. But *anytime* you are about to mail a letter, it is important to check it one last time to make sure your letter will be easy to read. So right now, let's take a minute to look back at our list of what makes writing easy to read. Use that chart like the checklist that the pilot used to land his plane. As I read each item on the list, will you check to see if you did it? Leave yourself a To-Do list if there is stuff you forgot." I read aloud the chart, which I had positioned at the front of the meeting area.

What Makes Writing Easy to Read

- spaces ("It isn't all scrunched together")
- neat ("Without a lot of eraser marks")
- a lot of letters in every word
- pictures that help
- hear lots of sounds in a word
- leave spaces between words
- make pictures that hold the words of the story
- use capitals at the start of a sentence
- use punctuation at the end of a sentence

"Writers, there is one more thing. When you write a letter, it is as if you're talking right to the reader. But instead of picking up a telephone, letter writers put their words on paper. If you say something on the phone that doesn't make sense, a person can say, 'Huh? What do you mean?' But when you write a letter, the person can't say to you, 'Huh? What do you mean?'

"So, before you send your letter to your reader, it's important to make sure that your letter makes sense so your reader will understand exactly what you want to say. Right now, Partner 1, will you read your letter aloud to your partner? Partner 2, your job is to listen closely, noticing parts that make you go, 'Huh?' Then you can work together to fix up those parts to make them clear. If we have time, you can switch." For a few minutes, the children worked together.

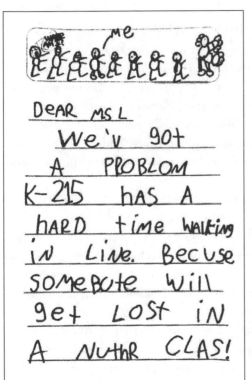

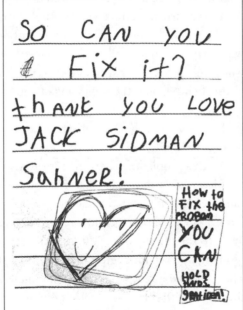

FIG. 8–3

Knowing Just What to Say

Angling Letters to Different Audiences

IN THIS SESSION, you'll teach students that when writers are working to make a difference, they write letters to many different people, angling those letters to the different audiences.

GETTING READY

✔ Chart paper and marker (see Connection)

✔ Students' writing folders (see Connection and Active Engagement)

✔ Shared class letter-writing sample, written to the grown-ups at the park, started in Session 7 (see Share)

✔ Clipboards, pencils, and revision strips (see Share)

COMMON CORE STATE STANDARDS: W.K.1, W.K.8, W.1.1, RI.K.2, SL.K.4, SL.K.5, L.K.1, L.K.2, L.K.6

Y OU'VE KICKED OFF LETTER WRITING with energy, awakening the little Lorax in each of your kindergarten writers. But you'll want to make sure that you continue across this second bend at the same pace as the last, inspiring your students to churn out letters with as much enthusiasm as when they made posters and songs, petitions and lists during the earlier portion of the unit. By now, each of your students will have written a small stack of letters. Your effort to actually mail some of these letters will surely propel your students into even more letter writing today and for the remainder of this bend. Collar the recipients of your children's letters and cajole them into sending speedy responses!

In this session, you'll teach writers that when they want to make a change in the world, it helps to find lots of people that can help. Ask writers to consider, "Who *else* could help me fix this problem?" Then encourage writers to compose more letters, persuading more people to join the cause. This will position you well to teach children to weigh how the same letter could sound to different readers, leading them to make similar material different. For example, a child writing to solve a problem with school lunch might write a letter to the principal suggesting a different menu. Then, later, he might write about this problem in a separate letter to his mother, suggesting he bring rather than buy his lunch. This time, he might write more informally, using terms such as yucky, and he might seal the letter with a kiss—something he is not apt to do in a letter to the principal! While both letters address the same topic, the voice, information and register change when the audience changes.

Again, it helps for students to imagine that the person to whom they are writing is standing right beside them so that they use an imagined conversation with that person as a way to rehearse what they want to say before writing those words down on paper. You might even engage the class in some writing-in-the-air, speaking in the voice of letters, to compose a class letter to fix a shared problem, such as a broken closet door or more books for the library, or a neighborhood cause, such as new sprinklers for the playground, filling cracks in the sidewalk, or installing a traffic light at the corner. In doing so, you'll support the standards for speaking and listening as outlined by the Common Core while also helping your young writers practice crafting thoughtful, structured letters.

"In this session, you'll teach writers that when you want to make a change in the world, it helps to find lots of people that can help you."

During your conferences and mid-workshop voiceovers, remind students to use strategies they've already learned for writing persuasively. For example, you might remind students that writing is more convincing if it contains reasons. Then too, children can be reminded that it can help to point out what the consequences might be if the problem is left unattended. As children learn to elaborate by providing reasons and evidence for their opinion, they will be far exceeding the Common Core State Standards for kindergartners. Way to go!

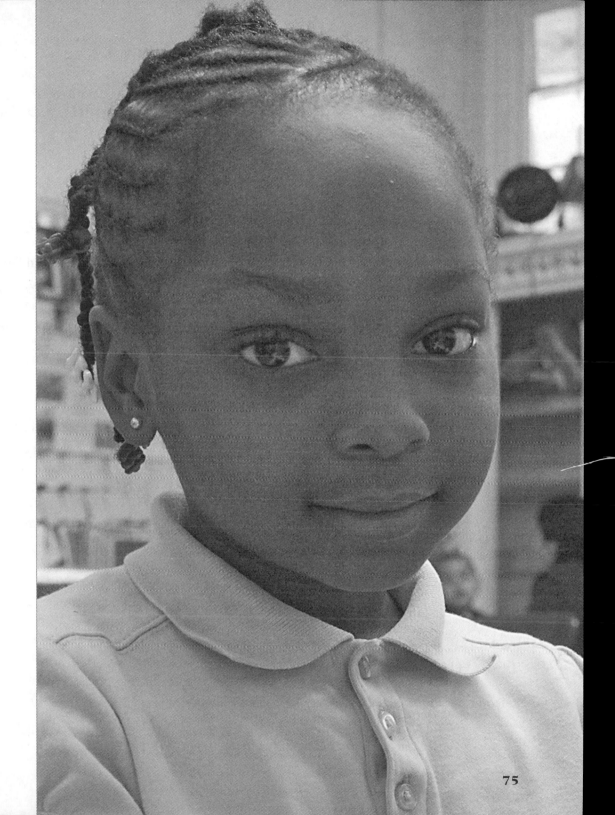

Knowing Just What to Say
Angling Letters to Different Audiences

CONNECTION

Tell a story about someone who adjusted his or her message—perhaps an ad—to suit very different audiences.

The students assembled on the rug with their writing folders in hand. "Last weekend, I took my dog for a walk through the park. It was a beautiful day and there were lots of people enjoying the outdoors. Then this teenager rolled into the park on his skateboard. He was holding a stack of fliers. I watched him roll up to a kid, hand him one of the fliers, and say, 'Come check out this skate park! You can practice cool tricks.' Then I watched him roll up to one of the moms to hand *her* a flier, too. I heard him say, 'You can bring your kids there. Don't worry, it's safe. There's rubber on the ground.' He skated around handing just about everyone a flier and telling them different things about this new skate park. He even gave *me* a flier, and told me that there was a doggy park next to where the kids skate."

Extrapolate the general point—that when wanting to reach someone, it helps to tailor the message.

"You know, that guy on the skateboard got me thinking about you and the work you've been doing in writing workshop. Because he didn't just give *one* person a flier and leave. He gave out *lots* of fliers to make sure that *lots* of people knew about the skate park, and he told each person the information that would be most important for them to know.

"If you want to really convince people to join you, you can't just write *one* letter. You'll need to write *lots* of them."

❖ Name the teaching point.

"Today I want to teach you that persuasive writers write *many* letters to fix the problems they see. They ask, 'Who *else* can help me fix this problem?' 'What do I need to tell *this* reader? Or *that* one?'" I scrawled the questions on the pad of chart paper as I spoke.

TEACHING

Referring back to an earlier letter the class helped write, generate plans for new letters to new readers.

"Earlier, we wrote a letter to the grown-ups at the playground, telling them about kids not playing nicely. We were trying to convince them to help make things better, to talk with the kids they brought, convincing those kids to play

◆ COACHING

Notice that when we begin a minilesson with a story, we keep it short and to the point. We don't want children to become consumed with skateboarding when our focus is letter writing.

Questions to Ask
- Who else can help?
- What do I need to tell **this** reader?

nicely. But if we want to *really* make things better, we need to write to more people about this, so they can help us fix this problem, too."

Gesturing to the chart paper where I'd just recorded two key questions, I said, "Remember that writers ask . . . " and the children chimed in as I tapped the pointer on the words.

"Who else can help?"

"So let's think about who else can help us fix the playground problem. Who should we write to next?" I paused to think quietly for a moment, too lost in thought to answer the pleading hands waving in my direction. "Oh, I've got it! We could write to the other kids at the playground! Maybe we could convince them to play nicely. Is that what you were going to say?" Some kids, who had been in the midst of an exasperated "I knew that! That's what I was going to say" sigh, chimed in that they had thought the same thing.

Then coach children to ask next, "What do I need to tell this reader?" and to tailor the message accordingly.

"So what do writers do next? After the writer thinks, 'Who else can help?' and decides on the person the writer wants to write, the writer needs to ask . . . " I pointed to the second question on the chart paper, and children joined in reading it aloud: "What do I need to tell *this* reader?"

"We could pretend the other kids were standing here and write, 'Boys and girls, I want to tell you that there is a problem at the park.'

"But wait. You kids probably *already know* about the problem, right. Remember how that kid at the park told the little boy that he could practice cool tricks and told me that there was a dog park near it—saying different things to different people? We better think about what we want our letter to all the other kids to say. It won't be the same as the letter to the grown-ups.

"So maybe we'll start it this way." I wrote-in-the-air.

> Kids, you probably already know that there is a problem at the park with kids not playing nicely. Will you help fix it?

I glanced back at the class for approval. "Better?" They assured me it was.

At some point before your next writing workshop session, you will want to craft this letter to the other kids, based on the ideas your students shared with you today. You will need this letter for Session 10.

ACTIVE ENGAGEMENT

Channel kids to think of the letters they wrote the preceding day and ask, "Who else could help?" and to plan more letters, tailoring them to the new readers.

"Yesterday you wrote letters to convince someone to help you fix a problem. But now you know that sometimes one letter is not enough! Writers need to convince *lots* of people to help make a change. Right now, please open your writing folders and take out the letters you wrote yesterday. Take a second to reread them." I gave them a moment to take out and reread their writing. "Now, think about the letter you wrote yesterday, make a plan for the letters you'll write next. You can ask yourself, 'Who *else* can help me fix this problem?' Then you can think about how your letter might sound different to somebody different. You can think," and I tapped under the words on chart paper as the children chimed in, 'What do I need to tell this reader?' Will you ask those two questions, in your mind, right now?"

I moved silently across the rug, listening in to children's plans, before crouching beside a partnership. By the time I reached Jessica and Tom, Tom had already told his partner that he'd written to his cousin, but that he wrote his cousin for no real reason. So Jessica pushed to learn the problem he wanted fixed. "I want to fix my room," Tom said. "I want bunk beds, like Kevin has!"

Tom had already written his mother, and so with Jessica's nudging, he decided he next needed to write his grandmother. Jessica approved. "Yeah, write a letter to your grandma," she said. "I don't think your cousin will be good at fixing your room."

I voiced over to get the partners thinking about audience, "How might your letter to your *grandma* sound different than the letter you wrote to your *mom* about the bunk beds? What will you tell your grandma to convince her to help?" Soon I'd reconvened the whole class and had recruited Tom to talk to all of them.

After explaining that he was going to write his grandma for help with bunk beds, Tom said, "I can ask her if she could pay for it with my mom so they could both get me one. And then my grandma could sleep on the bottom bunk when she stays over our house," Tom proposed. "So, let's pretend Grandma is right here next to you," I coached. "Pretend to talk right to Grandma to plan your letter. Dear Grandma . . . " Tom rehearsed, "Dear Grandma, Can you buy me bunk beds please? You can sleep on bottom one when you sleep over." I named what he had done that I hoped others had learned to do as well.

LINK

Send students off, reminding them that they need to write letters to multiple people, angling each letter to the new audience.

"Writers, I overheard you sharing ideas for all the letters you plan to write to convince, not just one person, but *lots* of people to help you fix the problems you see. Remember, whenever you finish a letter, don't stop and think, 'Job done!' You can ask, 'Who else can help me fix this problem?' and think about how that letter will go. You can think, 'What do I need to tell this reader? What is important for this reader to know?' to plan the letter you'll write next. Then you can go to the writing center to get started on another letter."

Questions to Ask
- Who else can help?
- What do I need to tell **this** reader?

This minilesson has a lot of dialogue for the children and of course there is nothing crucial about the particular things these children say. Your own class will have their versions of this.

Scaffolding Students Who Need More Support Writing Persuasive Letters

WHEN YOU TAUGHT YOUNGSTERS TO WRITE STORIES or how-to writing, you probably had a short stack of mentor texts that you carried with you as you conferred and lead small groups. That way, you had ready examples to draw upon for any quality of good writing you may decide to teach. When teaching better letter writing, this will be harder, because the world is not brimful of published letters. Make your own collection, then, or borrow ours, for a time. Lily's letter to her principal, Melanie, is on the CD-ROM.

If you are near a child when he or she is writing, coach that child to speak directly to the reader, explaining the problem, giving reasons why this has to be fixed, and telling the reader what he or she can do to help make things better. Perhaps you'll offer language stems that children can borrow, to verbalize their thoughts—chiming in and trailing off as a child composes the piece aloud. For instance, you might start a writer off, helping to focus ideas from the very beginning. "I'm writing to tell you that . . . " and gesture for the writer to keep your sentence going. Then, adding in as needed, helping a child elaborate along the way, say, "One reason is . . . " Or "I want to fix this because . . . " And later, "I think you should . . . " If these are written out for the child, they'll be a source of support.

But it is also okay if the child does not actually meet all your hopes. It is okay if some of the children's letters don't contain multiple reasons or aren't tailored appropriately for the particular reader. That is, this unit teaches kindergartners to do very ambitious work, and your hope is that they begin to gesture toward doing this work and that, with support, they begin to internalize what you are teaching. But you are not expecting anything close to mastery.

> ### MID-WORKSHOP TEACHING   Adding Important Details that Are Angled Toward Your Reader
>
> "Writers, can I have your eyes and ears?" I said. I waited until you could hear a pin drop. "Sometimes, it helps to ask yourself, 'What else does *this* reader absolutely need to know about this problem?' Remember, different readers may be more interested in different kinds of information. Remember how the teenager in the park saw me with my dog and then thought to tell me about the dog area at the new skate park? Think about what you can say to the reader you are writing that will really convince that particular person to help you. Then add those words to your writing so the person who receives your letter will understand how you feel and the important things you want."
>
> Don't forget, writers, that after you finish one letter, you begin the next. You'll be writing lots and lots of letters, and as you learn more, you'll revise the letters in the 'I'm done' part of your folders.

Persuasive Writers Include Big Feelings in Their Writing

Teach students that writers include their feelings about the problem they are trying to fix, to convince their readers to take action.

The students gathered in the meeting area with the letters they had been working on that day, as well as clipboards and pencils. "Persuasive writers include big feelings they have about the problem they are writing to fix. You can add how the problem makes you feel. Just like you put feelings in your true stories, you can include feelings in your letters. That way, you can convince the person who reads your letter to have the same feeling you do and help you make things better.

"Let's look back at the letter we wrote together to tell the grown-ups about the park problem." I reread the letter to the class. "How does all that make you feel? Turn and talk to your partner now." I gave them a few minutes to talk and then called the group back together. "So what are you thinking? What are your big feelings about what is going on at the park?"

"Bad behavior at the playground makes me really mad!" exclaimed Paul. "I mean, I always wait my turn to go on the slide, and then another kid cuts me in line, and they didn't even wait. That's not fair!"

"I get mad, too," said Kimani. "But I also get sad because some kids don't look around when they're throwing a ball and I get hit with the ball and get hurt. That makes me really sad, getting hurt."

"These feelings that you are having are very important to include," I said. "If your reader understands how you feel about your topic, they may realize why it's important to make a change. I will go ahead and add our feelings to our letter. I may have to use revision strips to fit it all in."

Channel children to reread the letter they wrote today and consider adding their feelings, using revision strips as you have just done.

"Now I'd like for all of you to reread the letter you wrote today and think about how you might add feelings to your writing. You can find places to tell your reader how the problem makes you feel. You might even add how you'll feel when things get better and the problem is fixed. If you need extra space to add feelings to your letter, I have revision strips here for you to use. So take a few minutes right here on the rug to do this work."

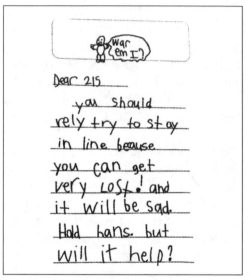

FIG. 9–1

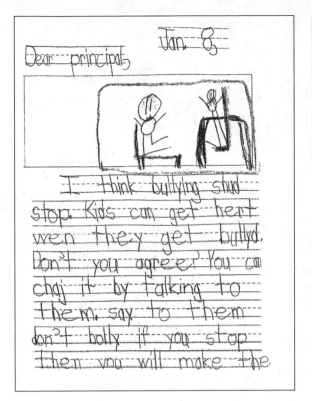

Jan. 8

Dear principal,

I think bullying shud stop. Kids can get hert wen they get bullyd. Don't you agree? You can chaj it by talking to them. say to them don't bolly if you stop then you will make the

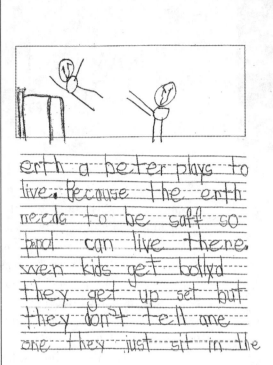

erth a beter plays to live. Because the erth needs to be saff so ppd can live there. wen kids get bollyd they get up set but they don't tell ane one they just sit in the

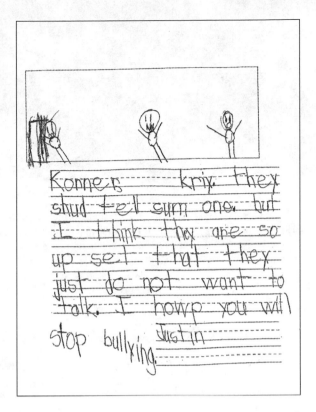

Konner, krix. they shud tell sum one. but I think they are so up set that they just do not want to talk. I howp you will stop bullying. Justin

FIG. 9 2

How Can We Make It Better?
Imagining Solutions

IN THIS SESSION, you'll teach students that persuasive writers include possible ideas for how to fix the problem they are writing about.

GETTING READY

✔ "We Can Be Really Convincing" chart from Session 8 (see Connection)

✔ Shared class letter-writing sample, written to the kids at the park, brainstormed in Session 9 (see Teaching)

✔ Students' persuasive letters, written in previous sessions to plan revision (see Active Engagement)

✔ Several student writing samples that demonstrate different strategies writers use in persuasive letters (see Mid-Workshop Teaching)

COMMON CORE STATE STANDARDS: W.K.1, W.1.1, RI.K.1, SL.K.1, SL.K.3, L.K.5, L.K.6

I N THIS SESSION, you'll demonstrate that writers seeking to address problems don't just list reasons why they want to fix a problem, they also add a way to fix it. This way, readers will know exactly what they can do to help. To support this elaboration and help children needing such help, including perhaps your English language learners, you might offer sentence stems, such as "Maybe we can . . ." or "We should try . . ." or even "I can . . ." By offering such supports, you'll help your children orally rehearse the words they'll soon add in writing.

You have probably noticed that the demonstration piece that resonates across the unit references a single topic: playing nicely at the playground. The work the class does to address this one problem unifies the work of the bend, providing a model that children can rely upon when they go and do their own independent work. This is the class topic—just as in *Writing for Readers*, the class worked on a story about a bumblebee flying into the classroom and during the how-to unit, the class worked on how-to texts, including how to make a peanut butter and jelly sandwich and how to have a fire drill. In each of those instances, the class topic and the class texts were not intended as topics or texts that every child needed to address during independent work time. In all these books, although the class text weaves in and out of many sessions, the children do not have a single topic or a single text that they persevere over for the entire week. By now, students will have likely churned out lots of letters, and those letters will have addressed lots of problems they want to fix.

You'll want to often remind writers to draw upon all they have learned in this unit, and in previous units. One way to do this is to prompt them to use classroom charts as checklists that guide them. Remember that it is always productive to ask writers to comb any new learning into their folder-full of past writing. That is, today's minilesson spotlights the importance of offering readers possible solutions to the problem, so you may want to suggest writers return to their folder full of writing and check that the letters they wrote previously all do this. This process of looking backward gives writers added practice with whatever the new strategy might be.

When teaching writers to suggest possible solutions for the problems they address, you may find that some five-year-olds have grandiose ideas for possible solutions. In their worlds, it may be entirely plausible to ask Mom to provide cleaner beaches. After all, she is a real-life superhero. In today's share session, you'll ask children to reflect on such monumental requests and think, "Is my suggested solution something my reader can *really* do?" This may help a writer understand that asking Mom to remember to bring an extra bag for garbage the next time they go to the beach would be a much more attainable solution than suggesting she clean up America's beaches.

"Remember that it is always productive to ask writers to comb any new learning into their folder-full of past writing."

Mahatma Gandhi famously said, "Be the change you wish to see in the world." You can help guide your children to follow this path, asking themselves, "What can *I* do to help fix this problem?" and considering ways they can help solve these problems and be the changes they wish to see.

How Can We Make It Better? Imagining Solutions

CONNECTION

Put today's work into context. Recall the observations the class compiled after studying a mentor letter, pointing out that the mentor author proposed possible solutions.

"Class, earlier this week, you studied the letter Lily wrote to her principal, suggesting ways to control noise in the school stairwells. Here is the list of things you noticed that Lily did in her letter that you could try as well."

"One of the ways Lily convinced her principal to take action was by giving her a suggestion for how to fix the problem. Remember, she said, 'Maybe we can remind the kids to not yell by putting a sign on the wall on every staircase.'"

❖ **Name the teaching point.**

"Today I want to teach you that persuasive writers suggest solutions to the problems they see. Writers include 'fix-it' ideas into their letters so that readers know possible ways to take action. To include solutions first the writer thinks of what the solution might be, and then the writer writes. First, you think of exactly what you want the other person to do, and then you write, 'Maybe we can . . .' or 'We should . . .' and include the solution right in the letter."

I added these sentence prompts to the chart—quickly writing them below "Give a fix-it idea."

Harking back to previous teaching—and a familiar class chart—helps remind students what they have already learned and prepares them for the new strategy you will introduce today.

We Can Be Really Convincing

- Tell your opinion
- Tell a little story
- Give LOTS of reasons
- Give a fix-it idea
- Maybe we can . . .
- We should . . .
- Be polite

TEACHING

Reread the letter you and the class wrote together earlier and recruit the class to help add suggested solutions to that letter.

"Let's reread our letter to all the other kids and think about how we could add a possible solution. Maybe we could use one of those phrases to get us started."

"We explained the problem and gave reasons why it is a problem. We even told a little story about a time when we saw this problem happen." I gestured toward the chart, showing that this was a form of checking off that we'd met expectations. "But I think, if we *really* want this to get better, we should add a fix-it idea so readers will know what they can do to fix this problem. Hmm, I'm wondering what people could do to fix this."

I left a moment of silence for all of us to consider possible solutions. Several children gave a thumbs-up signal to suggest they could offer ideas, but because I wanted every child to propose an idea or two, I said, "Tell each other the ideas you have for how kids could fix this problem."

I listened as children talked and then convened the group. "Jaden said he thinks kids should make sure to stop and look around before they throw a ball. That way they'll know if someone is in their way."

Sofia's hand shot up. "Maybe all the kids can learn to wait in line for the equipment, like wait for a swing, and not push ahead of someone who is already waiting."

I nodded. "We could add both Jaden and Sofia's ideas to our letter. By including possible soutions you make it more likely that your letter will spur the reader to act."

Later, I wrote these ideas on the enlarged chart-paper-sized letter (see following page).

ACTIVE ENGAGEMENT

Ask children to reread their most recent letter and check whether they proposed possible solutions. If not, ask them to work with partners to generate ideas for this.

"Go back to the most recent letter you have been working on, and will you reread it and a see if you have proposed a solution to the problem?" I gave the students some time to look back over a letter they had brought to the meeting area.

Then I voiced over, "Now, think about what your reader *might* do to fix it, and add that to your draft. You might write," and I used my pointer, tapping under these words so that children chimed in to read them in unison, "'Maybe we can . . .' or 'We should . . .' to get yourselves started." I left a moment for kids to generate possible solutions.

Dear Kids,

You probably already know that there is a problem at the park with kids not playing nicely. Will you help fix it? Sometimes kids get mad when they are waiting in line to use the slide and someone else cuts right in front of them. That is just not fair! One time, we saw a kid not look where he was throwing a ball and he hit a little girl right in the head. She was so hurt that she cried!

We should all play nicely at the park. Maybe we could try being patient and waiting our turn to use the equipment. And we should always look around before throwing a ball to make sure that no one is in the way and will get hurt. Let's try to play nicely together at the park.

From,

Class K-139

Speaking in a voiceover to channel the silent thinking, I said, "If you have thought of one way, see if you can think of another possible way to fix the problem." After a minute, I said, "Stop and jot. Start adding a solution to your letter." After a few minutes when I could hear the scratch of pens, I said, "Turn and talk."

Listen in as children write-in-the-air, voicing the sentences they could imagine adding to their letters.

I crouched near a partnership that I presumed would need some additional teacher support. "Zaara, what is your letter about?" Zaara stared, wide-eyed, back at me. "Who is your letter for?" I rephrased. "My mom," she replied. "What are you telling Mom in your letter?"

Zaara showed me that she'd written that she needed to stay up later. It made sense to me that she'd be stymied since there really weren't solutions to generate. The solution was clear: a later bedtime.

"I get it. You already told her the solution that you want—a later bedtime. Maybe what you need to do is to give her more reasons to say yes. Like you could promise her that if she says yes, then . . . What?"

Zaara was full of answers, and I encouraged her to add them to her letter.

LINK

Remind children of the full repertoire of things they should be working toward and then send them off to continue old letters or start new ones.

"Writers, remember that the big thing is to write letters that get your reader to do things that will help the world. You now know a lot of ways to do that. You can almost talk to your reader while you write. You can think of reasons that this particular reader will go for. You can suggest possible solutions. And today, whether you are finishing a letter you already started or writing a new one, do all those things."

CONFERRING AND SMALL-GROUP WORK

Remember the Predictable Architecture of a Conference

To HELP CHILDREN INVENT POSSIBLE SOLUTIONS to the problems they tackle, you might ask them to imagine a better way things could be done, zooming in on what would make the new way so much better, cleaner, safer, friendlier, or more fun. Then come up with a plan to make that way happen, using their knowledge of how-to writing to detail the steps.

When I pulled my chair alongside Anna, she had been working diligently, stretching words and recording sounds with impressive fluency. "Anna, what are you working on today?" I asked. "It's for my baby brother. He's zero. He keeps breaking all my toys," Anna explained.

"Will you read me the letter you've been writing?" Anna flipped her pencil around and tapped it across the page as she read (see Figure 10–1).

> Dear TJ
>
> Please do not break my toys. If you break my toys I will break your toys and Dad [will] have to pay his money. Please TJ ask mom or dad, ask mom or dad to fix your toys and then to be careful with the toys. Can you ask mom or dad? Can you ask sister or brother?

Plez do not Brak my toyz
if you Brak my toyz I will Brak
your toz and Papa have to pay he
meney poiz TJ Anak mamaor papa

② Pek at mama or papa to fix yourtoyz
and ther to be ktol with the toz
can you asxk mama or papa
can you asxk siftis or bathin

FIG. 10–1 Anna's letter

MID-WORKSHOP TEACHING   Celebrate Student Work

"Can I stop you all for just a moment?" I waited for pens to stop. Once I had all eyes in my direction, I continued. "I see that a bunch of you have figured out ways to make the letter you're writing even more convincing." I displayed Zaara's letter to share her work. "Zaara added fix-it ideas to her letter to her mom so that she'll let her stay up later." I projected another sample. "And here, Kevin wrote *more* reasons why the playground should have more trees and flowers. He had one reason, but he wrote *another* reason." I handed the letters back to the proud writers.

"Writers, I want to remind you that you can do this smart work with *every* letter in your folder! You can go back to find ways to make those letters on the red-dot side of your folder more convincing, too. Look back at our chart to decide what your letters might be missing that you might add onto right now. If you find something you need to add onto to a letter in your folder, mark it with a sticky note so you can remember to fix those letters up, too!" Students shuffled through their drafted letters, rereading and flagging letters to revise. I circled around the room to confer with tables, coaching this revision work.

SESSION 10: HOW CAN WE MAKE IT BETTER? IMAGINING SOLUTIONS   87

I leaned back and gasped. "Anna, you are doing things in your letter that are so convincing. One thing is that your words sound like you're talking right to your little brother, like he's right here next to you. And you are using polite words, like *please*. You even give TJ a reason why breaking toys is a big problem," I pointed to these lines out in Anna's letter. "I think that will help him understand why he should stop." Anna nodded. "The work you did here is something you should do in all your letters," I reinforced. "That way, the people you are writing to will understand *why* you want to fix these problems."

Notice, teachers, that I name what works in ways that are replicable and transferable, pertaining to other topics and other days. This turns the compliment into a strategy that students can draw upon again and again as they write, reinforcing the strengths they demonstrate and encouraging them to carry those skills across to other pieces. Also, writers within earshot will surely eavesdrop on this exchange and may take on these strategies to gain similar praise.

After giving a transferable compliment, I move on to teach a new strategy. By now I know that it helps if I explicitly signal that I want to teach something new. "Can I give you a tip to help you be *extra* convincing?"

Of course, there is no one tip that is especially perfect for this occasion. You could say, "Some writers find it can help to picture how things could be better if the problem is solved." I could then elaborate on how to do that.

Before the conference ends, it helps to recap the strategy in a way that helps children transfer what you've coached in one specific piece to the work they can do in any other piece. "So, Anna. Remember, when you're writing to convince someone to help you, you can picture how things will be better when the problem is solved and add that to the letter. Of course you can also write fix-it ideas to help fix the problem so that your reader will know what to do!"

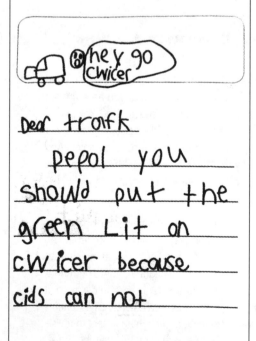

FIG. 10–2

Choosing a Letter to Mail

Give students an opportunity to read through the persuasive letters they have written, choosing one to mail.

"Writers, please bring your writing folders with you to the meeting area," I said, and when the children had all convened and put their folders down on the rug, I began.

"Writers, for the last few days, you have all been working so hard to fix the problems you see in the neighborhood. But no one is going to be able to help if your letters just sit in your folder!"

I continued, "We need to get these ideas out into the world! So tomorrow, we are going to walk right down to the end of the block and put our letters in the mailbox!" The kids smiled and cheered. "You'll have some time tomorrow to fix up your letters and make sure they are super readable. But, of course, what you need to do first is pick which letter you are going to send out into the world! So right now, please read through the letters that are in your folder and choose which one you would like to mail."

As children began to shuffle through their letters, I voiced over, "Don't worry if it is not quite done. You'll have time tomorrow to finish it up. What you want to think about is which topic that you've already written about is most important to you. Which problem do you want solved? You ready? Get to it!"

I circulated as the students reread, supporting those who needed guidance in choosing.

FIG. 10–3

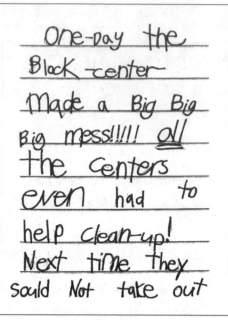

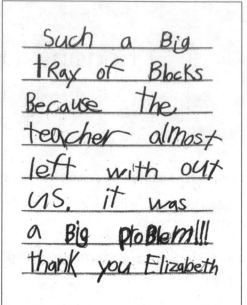

mr. peter

mr. peter
EVRY tHING
IS ON tHe
FLOOR !!!!!!!!

One-Day the
Block center
Made a Big Big
Big mess!!!!! all
the centers
even had to
help clean-up!
Next time they
sauld Not take out

such a Big
tRay of Blocks
Because the
teacher almost
left with out
us. it was
a Big problem!!!
thank you Elizabeth

FIG. 10–4   Elizabeth's letter includes an anecdote and a propsed solution for the problem.

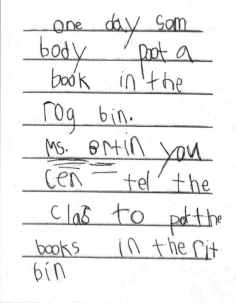

to Ms. Brtin
Bos are not
in the
rit bin.

one day sam
body poot a
book in the
rog bin.
Ms. Brtin you
cen tel the
clas to poot the
books in the rit
bin

FIG. 10–5   Michael decided to send his teacher a letter about a problem with the class library.

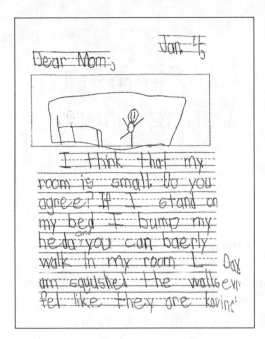

Dear Mom,   Jan. 4

I think that my room is small. Do you agree? If I stand on my bed I bump my hed. you can baerly walk in my room I am squushed the walls evr fel like they are kaving

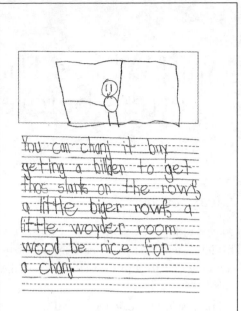

You can chanj it buy geting a bilder to get thos stuts on the rows a little biger rows a little wyder room wood be nice for a chanj.

My room is so small that a rat cant fits even a inch wepm cant fit in my room evr a butterfly cant fit in my room are you gunu chanj my room? yipy! thank you Justin

FIG. 10-6

Wait! What's That Say? Fixing Up Letters before Mailing Them

Dear Teachers,

Today is a day for celebration, because it marks the end of the second bend of this unit. This letter will help you create some instructional fanfare around the occasion, but it also leaves a lot up to your discretion. After all, you know your class and your context, and we don't.

The session is designed to end with a walk to the post office, or at least to the nearest federal mailbox or to the school's front office. Prior to this, the session provides you with a forum for teaching students more about fixing up their letters in ways that make those letters easy to read. That, of course, is an effort your students have been on about for a long time, and you will want to be sure to reference their earlier unit devoted to this purpose.

The Common Core State Standards' expectations for kindergartners are not especially ambitious. The standards ask that kindergartners "demonstrate command of the conventions of standard English capitalization, punctuation, and spelling when writing." More specifically, they are expected to capitalize the first word of a sentence or the pronoun *I* and record the phonemes of simple words, drawing on what they know about letters and sounds (CCSS L.K.2). Knowing this, you'll surely pay special attention to whether all of your children meet these standards, and you will want to provide extra help if there is a child or two who needs that help. But mostly, you will be teaching students to do work that is well beyond the standards. This is a good idea, because the demands of the standards escalate quickly in later grades, and giving children a head start makes sense.

MINILESSON

Your connection will remind children that letter writers need to check that their letters will be easy to read before mailing them out into the world. Remind them of strategies they already know for spelling as well as they can—checking the word wall to be sure this is not a word they know by heart, stretching words to hear and record all the sounds, remembering that every word and every syllable includes a vowel, using words they know how to spell to help them with words they don't know how to spell, remembering to separate words with clear finger spaces, and punctuating their sentences with the appropriate marks.

This sets you up to deliver today's teaching point. It is not an especially new one, so you will notice we suggest you speak of this as reminding children rather than teaching them. As you know, teaching points are designed to present children with not only the larger skill of *what* writers do, but also with an explicit strategy to explain *how* writers do this work. This language makes your teaching replicable, so children are better able to transfer the strategy to their own independent practice. Your teaching point could be worded as follows. "Today I want to remind you that writers check over their work carefully before sharing it with others, making sure it is clear and easy to read. One way you can make sure your writing is clear is to reread, looking especially for places that are confusing or hard to read. Then you can quickly pick up your pens to fix up those parts."

Now you'll be ready to demonstrate how to look carefully at a piece of writing to find parts that are unclear. You'll model how you look closely at each line of a letter, pointing as you read the words aloud. You'll probably decide to project a piece of writing or enlarge a page on chart paper so that students can easily see parts that are clear and parts that are hard to decipher. To do this, you'll want to have a piece with purposeful mistakes—ones that mirror the kinds of struggles you notice across the work of your children. Perhaps you've noticed that many of your writers do not use finger spaces consistently or that many forget to capitalize letters at the start of new sentences. Maybe in your assessments, you've found that students are capable of including end punctuation yet do not do so consistently. You might want to use this time to remind children to use the word wall to edit the spelling of sight words, or to include more phonetic sounds in unknown words. You might choose to rewrite a page of your demonstration letter to include some of these reoccurring errors. Or you might decide to share the work of a former student or make a piece of "kid writing" to share with your class, introducing it as the work of a young neighbor in need of their help. Whatever the case, this demonstration piece will house some of your kindergartners' common hurdles, and as you stumble upon mistakes in your rereading, you'll show kids your process for making those parts much easier to read.

Before inviting children to practice this during the active engagement, restate your process in a way that makes it replicable. That is, instead of saying, "Did you see how I listened for the middle sound of *rushing* and added *sh* to help make this word easier to read?" you'll say, "Did you notice how I listened not just to the starting sounds of words but to the middle sounds as well. Like I listened to all of *rushing* and noticed the middle *sh* was missing? Then I added the missing sounds."

During the active engagement, you'll want to give writers an opportunity to practice this process. There are a few choices for setting up this practice. You might choose to ask the class to help you with the piece in which you have done some modeling as well, reading on further into the piece, or you can turn the class's attention to a different piece or to their own.

Before sending your children off to work independently, remind them of today's teaching point and invite them to use this process whenever they are writing, not just today. Either in the link of your minilesson or during a mid-workshop teaching, you might decide to ask writers to look through all their letters, creating the same easy-to-read and hard-to-read piles that they created earlier this year. Of course, if you do this, you'll want to convey that the work should be quick, and be sure you usher your students to move into the work of fixing up their writing.

CONFERRING AND SMALL-GROUP WORK

The focus of your conferences and small groups will likely be on the spelling strategies and conventions you've determined need further support. You may coach students to reread their pieces, checking for specific word wall words and making sure they've spelled those words correctly. You might work with a small group to practice stretching out words they know are hard to read, listening for and adding more sounds across the word. You might differentiate the work for your more sophisticated writers, teaching them to use a capital letter not just for the first letter in the first word of a sentence, but also for dates and names—a Common Core standard for first-grade writers.

SHARE

Once you pull your writers back to the meeting area for the share session, you might say, "We have been working so hard to put our hearts and souls into our letters. Before we can drop these little pieces of our hearts into the mailbox, we want to make sure that these letters are easy to read so the people who get them can actually read them." Ask writing partners to work together, using a familiar checklist. Pairs can look across one another's letters to decide on ways to fix up a piece, making final edits together. Don't expect that your kindergartners will pinpoint each and every mistake or correct every misspelled word wall word. Their corrections will be approximations, and you'll likely find that even their fixed-up pieces have many imperfections. Celebrate the time and attention your young writers have spent on going back to a finished piece and their growing understanding of the purpose of doing so. This, in and of itself, is a victory!

Good luck!

Lucy & Liz

Draw on a Repertoire of Strategies to Write about a World Problem

IN THIS SESSION, you'll teach students that when writers want to tackle new, ambitious projects, they draw on all they know—in this case, all they know about writing persuasively.

GETTING READY

✔ A variety of paper choices including poster paper for signs, letter-writing paper, stationery for cards, poetry paper for songs, and narrative paper (picture box and lines) for petitions or opinion books for Writing Center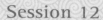

✔ A shared class topic—a social cause that you can write about across the bend. In this case we use environmental issues. (See Connection)

✔ "Writers Write to Make the World Better!" chart (see Teaching and Active Engagement)

✔ Chart paper and marker to record ideas for persuasive projects (see Teaching and Active Engagement)

✔ "We Can Be Really Convincing" chart (see Conferring and Small-Group Work, Mid-Workshop Teaching, and Share)

COMMON CORE STATE STANDARDS: W.K.1, W.K.5, W.K.8, W.1.1, RI.K.1, SL.K.1, L.K.1, L.K.2, L.K.6

THINK OF THE TIMES IN YOUR LIFE when you have been given a challenge that felt really huge, one that felt far beyond your reach. Focus on a time when the challenge was gigantic but you reached for it and accomplished more than you thought possible. In this final bend of the unit, we're imagining that you might want to give your children the gift of a similar challenge. We're suggesting that you rally children to write in ways that make a difference not just in their classroom, school, and home, but in the whole wide world, taking on issues of larger social consequence.

You are probably raising your eyebrows a bit at this inflated language and thinking, "These are kindergartners!" But remember that in their play, five-year-olds are very happy to rule the earth, to make mighty declarations, to create banquets. So the fact that this is a bit audacious is entirely age-appropriate.

We're suggesting that you channel children toward a shared cause—specifically, that you rally them to work to make the Earth a cleaner and greener place. They can extol the virtues of planting trees, recycling, picking up trash, avoiding pollution, and conserving water and electricity. You can fan the class's passion for this cause by reading a few books, watching a film, hearing a speaker on the topic, and perhaps doing all of that theme-based work before the unit even starts. In any case, we imagine that will occur outside the writing workshop. Once your class has begun to talk and think about the environment (or another cause), then your job will be to remind them to draw on all they have learned as they write on this topic. You may be surprised at the prospect of a shared topic—but there are no rules against whole-class, shared topics, as long as this seems to be the most powerful way to support students' growth.

In the days ahead, then, you will rally your students toward a shared cause of social consequence. By immersing your children in a real-world issue you help children write with knowledge and consequence.

We suggest that instead of continuing with the focus exclusively on writing letters, you return to the work from the start of the unit and again encourage children to write in all sorts of ways: petitions, signs, songs, and so on. The point will be that whatever the form of writing they choose, they are writing to persuade people.

Lucille Clifton, the great American poet, once said, "You cannot create what you cannot imagine," so we think it is important at the start of this final bend, that you imagine the work you are hoping your children will accomplish. Think, then, of an event, five or six days from now, in which your children will each stand before a large poster board containing a variety of writing and pictures. The children might each hold a pointer, just as they have seen you do countless times when you read aloud from a big book or from enlarged chart paper. And most importantly, each child has, seated in front of this display, an audience.

That audience won't be large, because youngsters will be more interested in performing than in listening appreciatively to other children, but the audience will be a forgiving one. You can decide if it contains mothers and fathers, grandparents, and assorted siblings, or if the audience is the custodian, the librarian, any free teacher-aides you can hustle up, as well as classmates.

"People," the child will say, "I want to tell you that . . . ," and then the child will launch into a soapbox speech in which he or she tries to convince others of something. The poster board will serve an important function in these speeches, because hopefully the poster board will contain key words, writing pieces, and illustrations that represent the main things children will talk about. As children talk about that main topic, they'll reference materials and read parts of their writing.

To prepare for this bend, you'll want to restock your writing center with baskets that again offer paper choices for signs, songs, lists, petitions, and letters. You may decide to clear out students' writing folders or perhaps supply students with new folders to collect pieces, across the week, which will soon comprise their persuasive writing projects. It'll be important to consider the volume of writing your children are now producing and to reflect your ambitious expectations in the differentiated paper choices you provide, offering more lines and stapled booklets, as needed.

Draw on a Repertoire of Strategies to Write about a World Problem

CONNECTION

Suggest that kids' interest in saving the Earth has convinced you that the class might tackle a shared topic. Suggest the class return to writing not only letters, but also signs, songs, petitions, and speeches.

"Writers, before yesterday, I thought our unit was going to be winding down and that we'd pick our best letter and then fix it up and fancy it up. But, after we talked about the way people are polluting our earth, I could tell that you all want to use writing to help not just your school and your town. You also want to use writing to try to keep the earth green and healthy. That's a very grown-up project.

"So listen. I have been thinking that maybe, just maybe, instead of winding down the unit, we could go for something really big and really, really challenging. *If* you are up for this, I was thinking maybe you could try to convince people to make not just our classroom and our school but the *whole world* a better place. Maybe we could write letters—and hey, we could make petitions and signs and songs and all kinds of writing—to convince people to help make the Earth cleaner and greener! And if we all work on this project together, we could help each other to do this work in ways that are better than anything we have ever done. What do you think?"

The kids erupted into cheers, quickly agreeing to join in the class pursuit.

❖ **Name the teaching point.**

"Today I want to remind you that when writers tackle new projects, they start by recalling all they already know how to do. If the project is writing to persuade people of something, writers think, 'What do I know about ways writers can write to make the world better?' Then writers go back and use what they already know how to do as directions to help them get started."

You'll see that we let kids in on the logic of our bends in a unit, helping them know the focus of a bend. By asking children if they are game for an ambitious endeavor, we recruit their dedication.

The way you talk, now and always, is as if one of the great joys in life is the opportunity to work with heart and soul on a project that matters.

TEACHING AND ACTIVE ENGAGEMENT

Show writers how to use what they know how to do as a guide for them proceeding forward. Coach them to identify a problem related to saving the earth.

"You already know that one way to remember all you have already learned is to look at charts in our classroom." I pointed toward the anchor chart that had been helpful earlier in the unit when students were generating their previous pieces.

"How about if we follow this chart, step by step, as we get started on a new project involving writing something that keeps our earth cleaner and greener?" I pointed to the first steps on the chart and the class chimed in.

1. See a problem.

"This time we are writing about ways to make the Earth greener and cleaner, so you need to think of a problem that relates to pollution, to cutting down trees, to things like that. Right now, turn to the two partners that are right next to you, forming a small group, and will your group talk about problems you see related to making the earth greener and cleaner. Talk about problems that writing could perhaps fix. Turn and talk."

I moved from one small group to another, getting behind the importance of children's concerns. They discussed garbage being thrown on the street, trees being cut down, and people wasting stuff.

Then I reconvened the group. "Before we read on, you need to know what problem *you* will be trying to fix. I heard some of you thinking about how there is too much garbage everywhere. Thumbs up if you were thinking about writing about that." I jotted that problem on chart paper.

"And I heard some of you thinking you might write about how too many trees are getting cut down to make roads and buildings. Thumbs up if you were thinking of writing about that." In that way, we created a small list of problems related to pollution.

Problems We See

1. Garbage everywhere

2. Cutting down trees

3. Wasting stuff: paper, water, electricity

4. People should ride bikes not drive cars

"Do you each have in mind the problem you will address?" I asked. "Show me, with your fingers, if you will be writing ways to solve problem 1, 2, 3, or 4?

Writers Write to Make the World Better!

We care a whole awful lot, just like the Lorax!

1. See a problem

2. Think

3. Write a lot!

4. Decide WHO?

"In a minute, those of you who are writing about garbage everywhere (problem 1) will sit here," I said as I pointed to one quadrant of the meeting area, "and those of you who want to talk about cutting down trees (problem 2) will sit there, I pointed to a second quadrant." Soon all the members of the class were sitting according to the topic they'd chosen.

After, ask members of the class to each choose a problem to address, reorganize seating so children are sitting with others who selected their topic. Channel these groups to invent solutions.

"Let's read on." Waiting until children's eyes were following the pointer, I tapped the second line of the chart and we read.

2. Think.

"How might you fix the problem of garbage everywhere or the problem of trees beng cut down? Or any other problems? Turn and talk." After a few minutes, I said "Let's hear from the group that's tackling garbage. Anyone have a way to solve your problem?"

I called on Sofia. "We could tell people to save their trash for when they get home and to not throw it out the car window," she said. Others added that some cars have trash bags hanging from the back of a seat.

"So then some of the members of this group might write a letter about not throwing trash out of the car? Who would you write it to? Or would you make up a song about it? And who would you sing it to? Will the rest of the class help them think this through?"

Again, the class broke into conversation. Soon the class had agreed that letters could be sent to parents, and signs could go under the windshield wipers of cars.

Debrief in ways that help all the children know how they can apply insights learned from every group to their own work.

"Writers, today and whenever you go to write something that you hope will make things better, you can do what this one small group just did and follow the steps on the chart. First, you think of a specific problem," and I motioned to that item on the list, "and then you think, 'How could people fix this problem?' Then think, 'What will we write, and who can help?'"

This is a new format for your minilesson, which is fitting for the third bend. You raise energy by convening issue-based study groups. Of course, all of this will be brief, but the impact on your children's zeal will be enormous.

LINK

Channel children to talk with their small group about the problem they're hoping to address and ways they think people could help to solve the problem.

"Right now, will all of you talk with your group about the problem you are trying to fix and what you might suggest that could help? Think what you will write, and who you will write to."

After children talked for a couple of minutes, I said, "Is anyone going to try writing a song to keep the Earth safe? Thumbs up if you are writing a song. Is anyone writing an announcement that you might read over the PA system, or some other place? Is anyone writing a petition that you are going to get a lot of people to sign? A book?"

"If you have a plan, off you go. Get started. If you are unsure, stay, and I can give you some extra help."

FIG. 12–1

Small-Group Work to Support More Theme-Based Writing

ALTHOUGH YOU DEDICATED TODAY'S MINILESSON to helping your students get started tackling a persuasive writing project, you will still have students in need of support. This writing may feel much less personal than previously when you rallied them to protest to stop tattling at recess or to advocate that Mom and Dad give you a later bedtime. For students needing support, you may want to keep them in the meeting area after others go off to write.

"Writers, I asked you to stay here in the meeting area for a bit longer because I thought we could work together to get started on some writing that will get people to take care of the Earth. I know the first thing opinion writers do is, one, see a problem. We already made a whole list of problems we've seen. So right now, let's work together to, two, think of a way to fix a problem. Let's think, 'What can we do to fix this littering problem?'"

"Oh! We should make sure people always throw their garbage in a trash bin," Tom piped up.

"Yeah, and recycle!" Shane called out.

I glanced back at the chart to address the next step, "We'll need to move to Step 3 and to write some idea (maybe a lot of ideas) to make things better. We could make signs, or make write a song make or a list. Wait! I know! Right now, let's get started on a petition, together, to help solve this problem." I selected a piece of petition-writing paper and paused to consider the final step. "But *who* is this petition for? Who needs to read this?"

The group was quick to respond, "Everybody!" "All the people that throw garbage." "People that don't recycle!"

"So if we're going to write something that convinces *lots* of people, we need to make sure it's really convincing." I pulled over the "We Can Be Really Convincing" chart and

---

MID-WORKSHOP TEACHING
Making Sure Proposed Solutions Are Feasible

For today's mid-workshop teaching, I wanted to bring the students back to the meeting area. "Writers, please bring the writing that you have been working on to the meeting area." Once students had convened, writing in hand, I began.

"Writers, today you have taken on a very big job—writing to persuade others to make the world a better place. We've been following this chart," I gestured toward our anchor chart, "to help remind us of the steps that persuasive writers go through. Remember, though, we also have our 'We Can Be Really Convincing' chart to help us, too. Let's take a look at that, now." I gestured toward the chart, reading through each item, but pausing when I got to this bullet.

- Give a fix-it idea

"Have you all been including fix-it ideas in your writing today?" I looked out and saw kids nodding eagerly. "I want to teach you that when writers write to help change problems they see, it is important that the fix-it ideas they include are things that people will *actually* be able to do. You have to make sure that your reader can *really* do what you're suggesting. If it is too hard, or even impossible, then he or she won't be able to help you fix the problem.

"Right now, go back to the piece you were working on today. Look back at a part where you've already added a fix-it idea, or right now, think about the fix-it idea that you can add. Ask yourself, 'Is this idea something my reader can really do?' Then ask, 'What can *I* do to help fix this problem?'"

I prompted the children to turn and share these ideas with partners, helping writers check for clarity and plan for elaboration. I walked around the room, listening in on the conversations. "Remember that when we write to make the world better, it helps to include ideas for how to fix things. It's important that we figure out how to help make it better, too!"

---

set it beside the small group to help the children recall strategies for persuading their audience. "I already know that it helps to explain the problem and your opinion right at the beginning. I better make a quick sketch to show this problem with littering and another quick sketch to show what we hope people will do, instead." I drew a simple before-and-after sketch at the top of the paper. Then I turned back to the group, eliciting ideas for how we might start our piece, before recording the first few sentences.

> Littering is a big problem. We see it in school, on the street, and at the playground. We don't like when people throw garbage on the ground.

"This helps to make sure people who read this know exactly what the problem is from the very beginning. But I'm not sure if it will *really* convince them, yet. What else do we know we can do to make this even better?"

"You have to put reasons and say, 'because,'" Maria prompted.

"And say, 'please' and 'thank you,'" Tom reminded.

I scrawled these additions quickly on the next lines of the page.

> We don't like littering because it makes the Earth dirty. People should recycle! Please sign this to help stop littering. Thank you.

Before I sent the students off to their own writing, I recapped the process and gestured toward the classroom charts, to help them transfer this work into their independent practice, coaching them to get started on their own pieces.

Sharing All You've Learned about Opinion Writing
An Interview

To celebrate the way children have drawn on what they already know about persuasive writing, suggest they have learned so much that a reporter should interview them. Then pose as that reporter and interview children.

As students gathered in the meeting area, I clipped the "We Can Be Really Convincing" chart to the easel as a reminder of all they are doing as opinion writers. Once the class was seated, I began.

"Writers, I can't believe how much you have learned about writing in ways that change the world. A reporter should interview you and then write a newspaper article about you."

I put on a fancy reporter's hat, some heavy-rimmed, ugly glasses, picked up a clipboard, and then held up an imaginary microphone. Making my voice gruff, I said, "I am Mr. Krockhow, a reporter. I have heard this class has learned a lot about writing to convince people to change the world. I'd like to interview each of you to learn about the kinds of writing you know how to do."

Shifting out of the role, I whispered to the class, "Turn and tell your partner what you will say to the reporter about how to write persuasively. Go!"

I listened as partners worked together. Then I convened the class and passed an imaginary mike from one child to another. With everyone watching, I approached Paul and said, "A-hem, sir, do you mind if I interview you?"

I held the imaginary microphone near Paul's mouth. He listened to the first question about writing to persuade people and launched into an explanation. "Well, see," he said. "The way it goes is that there's writing stories and there's writing other stuff like how-to books, and now we are learning that people write about problems." When the reporter pressed, Paul elaborated. The interview continued another minute or two, and then I moved on to ask a few other children to report their ideas.

"You need to put reason words, like *because*, and say why," Sofia named.

"You can say a little story about the problem, or you can put a fix-it idea," Gabriella added.

Taking off my reporter's hat, I returned to the role of teacher and said, "So, writers, you have become the kind of people who see problems in the world—and *do* something about them. You write! Remember to do this always, using all you now know about writing in ways that convince people to make things better."

You'll want to use every opportunity to keep the strategy charts in your room alive across the unit. This will serve to remind students as they collect new pieces and revise earlier drafts. Referencing these charts frequently will also continue to build writers' independence—using the room as a second teacher.

Chances are great that this will be one of your kids' favorite share sessions. If that happens, then you'll want to organize a think tank of teachers to find ways to adapt a few minilessons and shares so they engage children in similar ways.

Sound Like an Expert!
Teaching Information to
Persuade Your Audience

RECENTLY, ACROSS OUR STATE, a lot of people have been writing letters protesting the fact that standardized tests are becoming more high stakes. Some of those letters read like rants; others are filled with precise information that exposes the flaws of the tests and of the ways tests are used. It goes without saying that the highly emotional letters that are filled with exaggerations and emotion are less persuasive than those that are studded with well-researched, precise, compelling information.

Although it is unlikely that kindergartners will be able to research their topics well enough to embed lots of carefully chosen and compelling facts into their writing, this should not stop you from teaching your children that one of the most important ways to persuade someone is through the use of facts. If a child wants to try to convince people not to cut down the trees alongside her road, she would be wise to count how many trees are on her road now and to include that number in her writing. The youngster wanting to write about the importance of picking up garbage would be wise to describe the specific things he found when he and his mom picked up the garbage at the beach: 14 soda cans, 3 Styrofoam cups, and a plastic spoon.

Both this lesson and the one that follows it, then, teach youngsters the value of research and help them understand that research is not something fancy that scientists do in a laboratory. The writer who counts the number of trees or catalogs the kinds of garbage is doing research, and the precise factual information that the research yields moves writing toward being truly persuasive.

IN THIS SESSION, you'll teach students that persuasive writers make their writing convincing by including facts that teach their readers important information about their topic.

GETTING READY

✔ Student writing from previous session (see Connection and Link)

✔ Copy of Lily's letter (see Connection)

✔ "We Can Be Really Convincing" chart (see Connection)

✔ Example of student writing where information and facts can be added (see Teaching)

✔ Revision strips (see Teaching)

✔ "What Makes Writing Easy to Read" chart (see Share)

COMMON CORE STATE STANDARDS: W.K.1, W.K.2, W.K.8, W.1.1, W.1.2, RI.K.1, RFS.K.1, RFS.K.2, RFS.K.3, SL.K.1, SL.K.4, SL.K.5, L.K.1, L.K.2, L.K.6

Sound Like an Expert! Teaching Information to Persuade Your Audience

CONNECTION

Remind writers that texts can become teachers. Channel them to return to a text they studied earlier, this time learning from that text with more independence.

"Writers, will you come to the meeting area with the writing you did yesterday?" Once the children had settled, I said, "Writers, did you know that pieces of writing can be your teacher? It is true. Books and letters and songs that other people have written can teach you how to write.

"Do you remember earlier this year, when *My First Soccer Game* taught you how to write a how-to book? And earlier in this unit, Lily's letter taught you about things a writer can do to make writing that changes the world." The students nodded their heads in recognition.

Read the text aloud, leaving to children the work of naming what the author did that makes the writing effective and then applying those strategies to their writing.

"So right now, *I* am not going to teach you. Lily is! I am going to read her letter to you again. As you listen, think again about the things you notice that Lily has done that really work. Then I'll give you a chance to talk to your partner about what you noticed. Let's see if that letter can teach you again." I reread the letter aloud and gave the children a few minutes to talk.

After a little bit, I reconvened the class. "Many of you are talking about how Lily wrote her letter in a way that shows she really cared about what she was saying, and you are right about that. I've been trying to imagine whether her letter would have made a big difference if she had written it like this:

> Dear Melanie, I guess being noisy is kind of a problem. I saw it happen in the stairwell one time. It wasn't so good. You should probably make the kids be quieter. That's all. From, Lily.

"Instead, she wrote with a lot of passion and conviction, didn't she? She tried to show just how much she cared about this problem at her school. Each one of you, like Lily, will want to write in ways that will reach readers. It is like, as writers, you will need to stand tall and speak—write—loud and clear. And I know you noticed other things about Lily's writing as well.

Sometimes it seems that children learn something and then drop whatever they had previously learned. I think sometimes we are not aware that most of the things children do that make us shake our heads in despair are the direct result of our actions. If we want children to return to mentor texts, checklists, and concepts that we've taught earlier, then it is important to harken back to those. Your unit needs to be braided not only because strands cross into other disciplines, but also because one day's teaching crosses to another day's teaching.

It is often supportive to provide young writers with a contrasting example when studying a mentor text. By posing the alternative, by suggesting what the author could have written, students are quick to realize the strengths of the original.

"Now the hard part: will you look at your writing from yesterday and think about how you can do more of whatever it is that you admire in Lily's letter? We'll be really quiet while everyone thinks about that." I stared at Lily's letter, then at my own writing, modeling that I was so raptly involved in this that I couldn't check on the kids' work. After a minute, I said, "Tell your partner what you are thinking you could do to make your writing even better."

Children talked, and after a minute I said, "So you all are starting to have a list of ways you can make yesterday's writing a *lot* better, which is exciting. Today I am going to add one really important brand-new thing to your list of ways to make your persuasive writing even stronger."

✤ **Name the teaching point.**

"Here it is. The best way to make your writing stronger is to include important information. You can get that information by researching, which means looking closely, talking to people, asking questions, and reading. Then, you can include those details and facts in your writing. That's another way we can be really convincing." I added a Post-it with this strategy to the anchor chart.

TEACHING

Tell children about a child who reread his writing, realizing he'd included reasons for the problem and a suggested solution, and questioned if he'd included information.

"I want to show you the important work Diego did yesterday when he decided to add more information to his book. I am going to read you his book. You will notice that he included the reasons why cutting down the trees is a problem and he included a plan to fix the problem, but it is less clear whether he included a lot of precise, specific facts in his writing. See what you think."

> Don't cut down the trees. Don't! I will cry if you cut down the trees. One reason is because the trees are beautiful. I love them. I do not want them to die. Please don't cut them.

"What did you find?" I asked. Everyone agreed that yes, Diego had given reasons and suggested a way to fix the problem, but his letter did not yet contain a lot of information about trees.

Set children up to watch and join in as you and the child you describe think over how he can embed some information into his writing.

"The good news is that Diego actually knows a ton about trees. I've asked him to tell you what he knows, and then maybe Diego and the rest of us can work together to figure out how to get this information into his writing. These are some of the facts that Diego knows." I showed two facts, written on sentence strips.

> Trees are important because they stops the rain from washing all the dirt off the hill.

> The leaves of trees keep the earth cooler so we don't need so many air conditioners.

The connection of a minilesson is a time when today's teaching is connected to previous teaching at work. Usually it's the teacher who builds the bridges, but in this minilesson, the children are the bridge builders.

In this teaching component, notice that we are suggesting that you not only tell about how another child reread his writing, assessing it for these important dimensions, but that you also share the sequence of events in ways that recruit your class to do as the child did, assessing the writing for these important dimensions. That is, the teaching component of the minilesson not only tells children about the importance of doing some work; it also supports them in essentially doing that work.

"Let's think about whether there is a way that Diego could get that information into the writing. Let's take his first piece of information and work with that. 'Trees are important because they stop the rain from washing all the dirt off the hill.' Let's see, where does that fit?" I mused, turning again to his original writing.

> Don't cut down the trees. Don't! I will cry if you cut down the trees. One reason is because the trees are beautiful. I love them. I do not want them to die. Please don't cut them.

"Hmm. What are you thinking?" I thought, and then, as children watched, I added the first sentence strip into a place where it fit.

> Don't cut down the trees. Don't! I will cry if you cut down the trees. One reason is because the trees are beautiful. I love them. <u>Trees are important because they stop the rain from washing all the dirt off the hill</u>. I do not want them to die. Please don't cut them.

ACTIVE ENGAGEMENT

Recruit the children to continue the work of embedding information into a persuasive writing sample.

"Now, writers, let's work together to figure out where Diego could put this other piece of information. 'The leaves of trees keep the earth cooler so we don't need so many air conditioners.' I'll reread you what Diego has written so far and then give you a chance to turn and talk to your partner about where this sentence should go." I reread Diego's writing and then asked the children to turn and talk. After a minute or so, we reconvened.

"So? What do you think?" I waved the sentence strip in the air. "Where should Diego put this information?"

"I think that he could put it right after the part where he says that he loves trees," suggested Kimani. "Because maybe that's one of the reasons why he loves them, because they can be like air conditioners."

"Or maybe," volunteered Jacob, "he could put that sentence right after he says that he doesn't want the trees to die. He wants the trees to keep living because the leaves can be like air conditioners."

"Wow, writers, you have offered Diego some fantastic suggestions. Diego, you have a big decision to make!" I handed Diego the sentence strip, and he taped it into his piece, right where he wanted it. I reread his revised writing to the class.

> Don't cut down the trees. Don't! I will cry if you cut down the trees. One reason is because the trees are beautiful. I love them. <u>Trees are important because they stop the rain from washing all the dirt off the hill</u>. I do not want them to die. <u>The leaves of trees keep the earth cooler so we don't need so many air conditioners</u>. Please don't cut them.

Notice that here, and in many other teaching portions of minilessons, we set children up to begin doing a specific bit of work and then proceed to demonstrate how to do that work by doing the activity in front of them, sharing pointers as we demonstrate.

LINK

Ask children to think about precise information to incorporate into their writing before you send them off to write.

"Writers, now it's *your* turn to incorporate information into your persuasive writing. Just like Diego added some of what he knew about trees into his writing about saving the trees, you can go ahead and include what *you* know about *your* topic into the writing you've been working on. Remember, this information, the facts that you know, will make your writing more convincing. And the more convincing your writing is, the more likely people will be to take action and help you!

"Reread the writing you wrote yesterday. Then turn to your partner and talk about some information that you know about your topic and see if the two of you can figure out how you can add that information to your piece. Remember, think about *all* that you know about your topic. Think about the books we've read together, the pictures that are around the classroom. All of these things are places where you can get information for your writing." I gave the students a few minutes to talk, listening in on bits and pieces of their conversations, and then called the group back together.

"I noticed that many of you have ideas about information you could include to make your writing even more powerful."

Recruit one child to show her work to the class, telling others how she plans to insert information.

"Bailee, can you share with the class what you were thinking about, with your sign about littering?" Bailee joined me at the front of the meeting area, holding up her sign for all to see (see Figure 13–1).

> Do not throw garbage on the floor because the earth will be all sticky and it will be all garbage. Ok?

"I made this sign about littering. People should not throw garbage on the street. I think that I should add information about how garbage on the ground makes animals sick. Because one time me and my dad were walking my dog and he ate some garbage that was on the ground, a chicken wing. And then a little bit later he got real sick and threw up."

"Fantastic idea, Bailee! And remember, writers, when you finish the writing that you are working on, you can write *another* piece, maybe a song, a petition, maybe even another letter. There are *tons* of things to write about to convince people to help you make the world a cleaner, greener place.

"Those of you who feel ready, off you go! And if you are having some trouble coming up with information to include in your writing, stay here in the meeting area, and we'll do some work together to figure out how to come up with information to make your writing really, really convincing."

FIG. 13–1 Bailee's sign included reasons that call people to action. She then made revision plans to add important information to her sign.

Animils can get sik

FIG. 13–2 Bailee's first revision strip

You may notice that this minilesson doesn't really equip writers to do all the dimensions of this activity. The minilesson helps children embed information into a text but detours around the question of how children get that information in the first place. Our assumption is that the information students are including is mostly based on prior knowledge and personal experience.

Helping Students Find Precise Information to Incorporate into Their Writing

WHILE IT IS IMPORTANT that students are including information in their writing, the focus of this unit is not on research writing. Most of the facts your children will be incorporating into their pieces will come from the books you've read aloud on your shared topic, video clips you have watched together, and guests that may have come to speak. That is one of the reasons why you have rallied your class around a shared cause. By limiting your students to a broad umbrella topic, you are able to support their developing knowledge of that topic. Students need not go to the library and find their own books and then work their way through them, distilling the most important information. You can do that distilling for them. You have prepared them for this kind of persuasive writing by reading aloud many books on your topic. Perhaps you have left photographs all around the classroom. Or you have filled your independent reading library with nonfiction books on the topic. Because of their immersion in the subject at hand, it should not be a tremendous challenge for your children to recall facts that they will incorporate into their pieces.

However, regardless of all of your careful preparation, there will still be some students in your class who find it difficult to recall the kind of precise information that is necessary to make their writing more convincing. They may need more support from you. At the end of today's minilesson, you asked students who were struggling to come up with information to stay in the meeting area. Perhaps you will take this opportunity to work with this small group, helping them to find this information. Maybe you will reread one of the books that you had read aloud prior to this bend. As you are reading, ask children to give you a thumbs up when you read something that is very, very important. You can record this information on a piece of chart paper for your students to use as a reference when going back to their independent writing.

Another option is to lead the small group in a discussion on the topic. Your students probably know more than they realize about keeping the earth cleaner and greener. Just by allowing them to talk to each other, hold court, and share ideas, more facts may bubble to the surface.

After you help the children come up with the information they need, you may want to walk them through the steps to incorporate that information into their writing. You can use one student from the group as a model. Reread the student's writing, and ask the others to help that student find the appropriate places to insert this new information. And finally, before you send the students off to work independently, you may want to make sure they have a handle on how they will be incorporating the information into their own writing. Be sure you remind them that they can use Post-its or flags or code-inserts to add information into a text.

MID-WORKSHOP TEACHING
Writing Partners Can Be Mentor Authors, Too

Standing in the middle of the room, I asked for children's attention. "Writers, earlier today you learned from studying Lily's letter. Right now, I want you to get together with your partner and put *your* piece of writing between the two of you. And this time, will you learn from each other's writing? Do just what you did with Lily's writing, and star the things that your partner has done that will make it really convincing. Then you can look at your own writing and see if you can do that, too."

As writers worked, I voiced over. "Use your most careful eyes to read each other's writing and think, 'What did this writer do that makes this writing really convincing?' See if you can take lessons from your partner's writing!" After a bit, I channeled children to resume their writing, this time with new work on their To-Do list.

Checking Writing for Readability

Remind students to use an anchor chart to double-check that their writing is easy to read.

I circled the room while the children worked at tables, quickly taking an inventory of the levels of writing students were in the midst of producing. Then I paused the students. "Can I have your eyes and ears for a moment? You've been very busy working on ways to make your writing really convincing so that *lots* of people will help you make our Earth better. But remember, writers, you also need to make sure your writing is easy to read. If people can't understand what you are trying to say, they'll *never* be able to help you!" I gestured toward a chart hanging near the writing center. "You can look back at your pieces and check to make sure you use what you know to make your writing easy to read. I'll read these over, and then will you look at whether you have done these things?"

What Makes Writing Easy to Read

- spaces ("It isn't all scrunched together")
- neat ("Without a lot of eraser marks")
- a lot of letters in every word
- pictures that help
- hear lots of sounds in a word
- leave spaces between words
- make pictures that hold the words of the story
- use capitals at the start of a sentence
- use punctuation at the end of a sentence

"Right now, look back at the piece you have written and decide what you could do to make it even easier to read. You can fix those parts up and remember to do this always as you keep going with your work."

More on Adding Detailed Information to Persuasive Writing

ear Teachers,

We're suggesting that yesterday's message is so important that you devote a second day to the importance of writing with precise, detailed information. Before actually planning the minilesson, it will probably help you to think carefully about what you imagine your students' work will be today. There are only a very few days left in this entire unit, and before long, you will want every child to be in a position to stand alongside a poster board, pointer in hand, and deliver a little speech in which the child talks about the main points he or she wants to make. So what do you expect your children will be working on today, tomorrow, and the next day?

Thus far in this unit, you have tended to convey the image that kids are working like crazy to crank out more and yet more pieces of writing. Initially those pieces were characterized by variety. Children wrote on varied topics, in varied genres. Then for a time all the pieces were persuasive letters. Now writers are again encouraged to write a variety of kinds of texts and a variety of topics—all related to the larger cause of protecting the environment. Without actually spelling this out, you have angled the kids to each write a piece of writing related to this theme, and then to return to that piece of writing so as to make it better by incorporating both features from a mentor text and more information into the draft. So now what?

If today's lesson teaches writers more about researching for information and inserting it into pieces of writing, you need to decide whether you imagine that all writers will search for more information that relates to the text they have been working on. That would be very challenging work for your students to do. They have already picked the low-hanging fruit, inserting the information they could find most easily into those pieces. So although it would be ideal for students to revisit those pieces yet again, chances are good that if you channel all your students to do this, many of them will become paralyzed and need your help.

COMMON CORE STATE STANDARDS: W.K.1, W.K.2, W.K.8, K.1.2, RI.K.1, SL.K.1, SL.K.6, L.K.1, L.K.2, L.K.6

So we suggest that you start this minilesson by reminding your students that writers don't just write one piece on a topic of concern and then be done with that topic. You will encourage children to move from one piece of writing to another. That way, children will all have something productive to do, whether or not they can find information to add to their writing. They also will soon have new texts that will require yet more information.

MINILESSON

You might start by appreciating the fact that some children are done with the writing they have been working on. You could say something like, "Writers, I notice that many of you are done with your first piece about taking care of the earth. How many of you also remembered to reread your writing and to find ways to make it even better, perhaps by adding information, before putting it away?"

Then you could remind writers that they can write more than one piece on a topic. Remind them that to make real changes in the world, it is important to write many different pieces to address many aspects of the topic. You can refer to the "Writers Can Make a . . ." chart from Session 3 and help your students imagine the possibilities for other kinds of writing they can do on their topic. Guide them toward the variety of paper choices they have available to them. Of course, it is ideal for children to work for a long while on one piece of writing, if they actually are productive, so you might find a way to acknowledge that.

You will need to decide what you want to teach about adding information to a piece of writing. You might suggest that books can teach children specific information about their topic. "Writers, today I want to teach you that if you want to be sure that whatever you are writing is filled with lots of precise details, it can often help to read a bit about the topic you are writing about."

Another angle you take could be about the kinds of information students should be adding to their writing. You could say, "When you are adding information to your writing, it helps to remember that precise names and numbers and colors matter."

Now you will want to demonstrate how you do this in your own writing. You probably do not want to create a whole new text, because then it will be hard to spotlight the one thing you want to teach. You could continue to work from Diego's writing about saving the trees. Or perhaps there is another student whose writing the class has come to know, via mid-workshop teachings or shares. Whatever you decide, do a quick reread of what has already been written, and then you can move on to teaching the new strategy.

If you are demonstrating how writers read to find out information, you may want to begin by thinking aloud. You could do a voiceover, saying something along the lines of, "Hmm, I know I need more information about how important trees are, about all of the great things they do for the environment. I better be on the lookout for this kind of information as I'm reading." Then read aloud, stopping to narrate. "Wow, this seems important to know: trees provide homes for all sorts of wildlife. I bet that fact will help me convince my readers that we need to save the trees." Model how you put a Post-it on this page so you can go back and find the information when you are done reading. Perhaps you will read on, finding one more fact. Don't finish the book, though, because you will want to give your students a chance to read and find facts during the active engagement portion of your minilesson.

If you are teaching into the second point, about precise details, you may want to share with the class a sample of writing that does *not* include any precise information. Put up a bare bones example of persuasive writing, one that does not include any facts. Similar to what you did with Diego's writing in the previous session, you can prepare several sentence strips with facts to embed in that writing. Be sure that a few of the sentence strips are ripe with detailed, specific information and that several of the sentences are crafted with very general information, in a direct contrast to the others. Think aloud about which sentences will enhance your writing, which sentences will be more convincing to your readers. Again, do not complete this revision work, since you want to give your students the opportunity to try it out during the active engagement.

Now it is time for your students to give this a try. If you have been teaching the first point, that writers read about the topic they are writing about and look for information to include in their own writing, read on. Ask your students to give you a thumbs up when you read precise information that could go into the writing sample. When they give you the thumbs up, pause and allow someone to explain why this information is important, why it will help to make Diego's writing more convincing.

If you have been teaching toward the second point, now it is time for your students to make decisions about which of the sentence strips that you have prepared will enhance the writing. You can ask them to turn and talk to a partner, making choices not only about which sentences have precise information to be included, but where the information should go. As with the other teaching point, be sure to have students explain why they are making the decisions they are making. It is important for writers, even at this young age, to be able to be purposeful about revision.

Before you send students off, you can scaffold their independent work in several ways. If you have been focusing on reading for information, perhaps you will give students an opportunity to look through the bins of nonfiction independent reading books, searching for a book on their topic. Send them off with their books and a stack of Post-it notes so they, too, can note important information as they read. If you have gone with the second teaching point, maybe you will ask your students to look over their writing from the previous day. Have them reread, looking for places where they can make their writing more precise.

Regardless of what you have taught, be sure that before your students leave the meeting area, you remind them of the strategy, in very general terms. You might say something like, "Remember, writers, *anytime* you are writing persuasively, it is important to. . . ." Transference of your teaching point to many pieces of writing, many days, is crucial.

CONFERRING, SMALL-GROUP WORK, AND MID-WORKSHOP TEACHING

If you have focused today's minilesson on reading to find important information, your conferences and small-group work may feel more like they belong in a reading workshop than a writing one. You may be noticing that in a fit of Post-it enthusiasm, your writers are noting important information on every page in the books they are reading. They are not necessarily reading with the lens of "What information is most important to include in my persuasive writing, and which information will help me persuade my readers and call them to action?" You may need to pull a small group, reminding students that when reading non-fiction to determine what information is most important they need to first think about their purpose for reading. In this case, it is to find information that will help persuade their readers. Help them come up with a question to guide their reading. With a guiding question, their reading will become more focused and purposeful—and the Post-its, more meaningful.

Some of your students may be struggling with determining whether the information they have included in their persuasive writing is precise or exact enough. It is easy for a five-year-old to say, "You should separate your recycling from your trash. There are lots of different things that get recycled." It may be harder for them to elaborate on the different kinds of materials that get recycled. It will be important in this conference, and every conference, that you not just work to "fix" today's writing, but that you give students a strategy they can use for the rest of their writing lives. Name this strategy. "Writers need to include detailed information in their persuasive writing. Detailed information will help your readers know exactly what the problem is you are looking to have them help solve. Detailed information can also help your reader fix the problem." In the case of recyclable materials, you can coach the writer into going into specifics about the different things that get recycled. Cans? Newspapers? Magazines? As they add this precise information to their writing, you may want to explain to them that now, because of their writing, not only do you know that you need to separate your garbage from your recycling, but you also know *exactly* what it is that you need to pull out to recycle. And now, you too can help out and make a difference! All because of their writing!

Because of all the hard work your students are putting in today, doing research reading, determining important information, and then embedding this information in their own writing, you may decide not to pull the class back together for a formal mid-workshop teaching point. You may instead decide to simply do a few mid-workshop voiceovers, highlighting students who are working at this efficiently, pointing out precise information that is being included in the writing. Keep the flow of the writing workshop moving along. This is challenging work that you are asking of your kindergarteners. Keep the momentum going.

SHARE

For today's share session, perhaps you will have several students who tried out the strategy that you taught now share their writing with the class. It will be important that they not only read the new, improved, information-rich writing, but that they also read the *before* version as well. Give their classmates a chance to reflect and ask questions. Highlight for the class how much more powerful and persuasive the writing is that is rich with precise information.

Enjoy!

Lucy & Liz

Writing How-To Books to Make a Change

IN THIS SESSION, you'll teach students that writers can write how-to books to give their readers detailed instructions about how to solve a problem.

GETTING READY

✔ "How-To Writing" chart, from the *How-To Books* unit (see Teaching)

✔ Stapled booklets for how-to writing, picture box and space for each numbered step (see Teaching)

✔ Student writing folders (see Active Engagement)

✔ "Writers Can Make a . . . " chart (see Link)

✔ Example of student writing that models the work of adding suggestions and warnings (see Mid-Workshop Teaching)

✔ Students' current writing and revision pens (see Share)

COMMON CORE STATE STANDARDS: W.K.1, W.K.2, W.K.5, W.1.1, W.1.2, RI.K.1, RFS.K.1, RFS.K.2, RFS.K.3, SL.K.1, SL.K.3, SL.K.4, SL.K.5, L.K.1, L.K.2, L.K.6

THROUGHOUT YOUR TEACHING, you will often want to hearken back to skills and strategies that children learned earlier. As in previous units, in this unit your students have continued to learn from mentor texts and to use checklists to self-assess and to plan for future writing. Additionally, partners have continued to be used as preliminary readers, asking questions of and giving feedback to writers, to tighten up and enhance their writing. However, today's session draws on prior learning in a different way. Today you literally suggest that sometimes when writing persuasively, writers can incorporate other genres into their persuasive project. More specifically, writers will learn to incorporate how-to texts.

In adult writing, a single text will turn corners, becoming at some points more procedural and at other points, more narrative, We do not expect that sort of control is within reach for many kindergartners, but we do think a five-year-old who has been writing about the need to keep the earth green by planting trees might shift, one day, and write a book titled "How to Plant Trees."

Before teaching this session, you may want to remind yourself of the teaching points from your how-to unit. You can remind yourself and remind your children all at one time by fetching the charts you made during that unit and bringing them into the center of your meeting area.

You'll probably choose to direct your mid-workshop teaching to the work of helping your children recall the strategies they learned during the how-to writing unit. During today's share session, you'll ask any writer who did make a how-to book to share their writing. As children read each step aloud, you can coach listeners to ask, "How?" or "Where?" or "What?" in ways that nudge writers to explain that step with greater detail, adding descriptors like *carefully, in the recycling bin,* or *plastic* bottle. That sort of nudging can help a child go from writing lines such as "Throw it out" to writing, "Throw out the plastic bottle in the recycling bin, carefully." This supports the expectations of the Common Core State Standards for Speaking and Listening that ask kindergartners to participate in collaborative conversations with peers and adults, asking and answering questions to get more information and seek clarification.

Writing How-To Books to Make a Change

CONNECTION

Remind students that for their writing to be truly persuasive they should provide their readers with a possible solution to the problem they are writing about.

"Writers, I know that some of you have been working together on a petition to help fix the problem of littering. People are throwing their trash in the wrong places, like on the floor or in the streets. I want to remind you that if you *really* want to make sure you solve this big problem, you need to not just complain about the problem but also give people steps to fix the problem.

"You already know that persuasive writers need to have some solution in mind and to be calling out to readers, saying 'This way! This is a good idea!'"

❖ **Name the teaching point.**

"Today I want to teach you that when you explain your solution to readers, sometimes it helps to do that by writing a how-to book. After you think, 'What should people do to fix this problem?' you write every step in a way that teaches readers *exactly* what to do."

TEACHING

Refer students back to the "How-To Writing" anchor chart.

"I know some of you have been writing about how to solve the problem of littering, especially littering that happens along the road. People throw their trash out of their cars. Maybe if we write a how-to book about this, people will be more likely to take action, to stop throwing trash out of their cars. Because not only will we have told them all about the problem, but if we write a how-to book, we will give them an idea of how to *fix* the problem!" The children nodded their heads in agreement.

◆ COACHING

It is helpful to teach writers the conditions under which they'd choose to use a strategy. This connection does that it says, "If…, then…."

Because you have already taught children how to write procedural text, you can now call to mind an armload of strategies and tips, just by saying the term How-To *book.*

After a few seconds for thinking, I said, "We really need a solution, don't we? We need a way to fix the fact that people throw trash out of their cars. Hmm. How about if we teach people how to hang a trash bag over the back of their car seats? And then use this bag to get rid of the garbage they have in their cars. Does that seem reasonable?" A chorus of yeses rung out around me.

"Think with me: what do we need to do first to write a how-to book about littering. Wait, I have an idea. Let's go back to our 'How-To Writing' chart."

How-To Writing

1. Tells what to do, in detailed steps.

2. Numbers the steps.

3. Has a picture for each step.

4. Has labels that teach.

Model the steps to take in writing a how-to book.

I pulled out a familiar how-to writing booklet and proceeded to plan the steps across the pages as I touched each page to tell each step. "Okay, so the first thing I need to do to write a how-to book is to tell my reader what to do, in detailed steps. So let's see, step 1: Get a paper bag with handles. Step 2: Hang the bag over the headrest of the front seat. Step 3—hey, that's going to be an easy one! Step 3: Put your garbage in the bag. Step 4: Take the bag out of your car, close it up, and find a garbage can to throw it in."

Debrief by naming what you did as a writer.

I turned my focus back toward the class. "Writers, did you see how I did that? I decided on a fix-it idea to teach people how to fix this problem. Then I planned out all the steps, one at a time, so readers will know how to fix this problem. By writing a how-to book, not only am I telling my reader *what* to do to fix the car littering problem, but I am telling them *how* to do it. It's like there is no way for them *not* to help, since they know exactly what they should do!"

ACTIVE ENGAGEMENT

Channel students to think of a possible fix-it idea for a how-to book by rereading the writing they have already done.

"Writers, you all have your writing folders with you. What I'd like you to do right now is take a few minutes and read over the writing you have done for the last few days—all of the writing you have done to persuade people to make the

Earth a cleaner, greener place. See if there is a problem that you have been writing about that you could think of a fix-it idea for. Show me a thumb when you have a fix-it idea ready!" As students reread, I made my way across the meeting area, guiding students who were having some trouble coming up with fix-it ideas, nudging them toward possible solutions. I moved back to the front of the room and reconvened the group.

"Okay, writers, I see plenty of thumbs. Right now, take a few minutes and turn and talk to your partner, telling them about your fix-it solution. Tell them the steps they'll need to do so that they'll know *exactly* how to make things better. Just like when you wrote your how-to books, use detailed steps to teach your partner what to do. Remember to teach your partner what to do first, second, third . . . " I trailed off as kids started to talk to their partners.

ACTIVE ENGAGEMENT

I moved near a partnership to listen in. "I could make a how-to book to teach people to ride their scooter instead of going in the car," Jonathan suggested. I nudged his partner to ask what to do first.

"First, put on your helmet. Then get your scooter. Then, put your foot on and push." I prompted the partners to switch before moving to another pair.

Kevin was listing steps across his fingers. "First, you turn the faucet off. Second, check it to make sure it's tight. Third, wait to see if it drips and if it drips then it means there's a leak and you could waste water."

"Yea and then you have to call your Dad to fix it," Summer added.

"That could be step 4!" I encouraged.

LINK

Use the "Writers Can Make a . . . " chart to help students make a plan for the kind of writing they will be doing.

"Writers, the idea of writing a how-to book to go with your topic is just one idea for what you could do today. You could do that today, or you could do something different. If you look back at our 'Writers Can Make a . . .' chart," and I gestured toward it, "you can remind yourself of all of the possibilities for your persuasive writing today!" I reread the chart to remind students of the work they could be doing, quickly adding "How-To book" to the menu of options.

"Okay, everyone, take a minute and think about what kind of writing you are going to be doing today." I paused for a moment. "You all ready? Okay, if you are going to be working on a how-to book, head off!" After the how-to writers were sent off, I continued on. "If you are going to be making a sign, get to it!" I let the sign makers head to their independent writing and continued on down the list, sending students off to write based on the type of writing they would be working on.

Using the Opinion Writing Checklist to Assess and Create Small Groups

ARLIER IN THE UNIT, you asked your students to use the Opinion Writing Checklist to self-assess. They read over their writing and used star stickers to mark places in their writing where they had demonstrated an aspect of the checklist and they used those same stickers directly on the checklist to signify areas that needed improvement. You will have used the checklist as an assessment tool as well. As you study students' work in relation to the checklist, you will find groups of children who need similar help. This is the perfect opportunity to create small groups to support those children.

For example, you may find that a cluster of children seem content to write with just a single reason. They state their opinion, give a quick reason, and then seem to feel that their job is done. You may want to pull these students into a small group. You could teach the group that one way to generate a more convincing piece is to consider the consequences as if people don't do the recommended actions. Teach them to ask, "What if …" questions. To demonstrate this, you could perhaps choose one student to

---

MID-WORKSHOP TEACHING   **Adding Warnings and Suggestions to Persuasive Writing**

"Writers, eyes on me, please. I want to show you something really cool that Alyssa did in her letter to her mom and dad." I displayed Alyssa's writing (see Figure 15–1). "Check this out! She added a suggestion to her letter. She suggested something her mom and dad could do to help recycle. See, right here!" I pointed out the line in Alyssa's writing. "She says, 'You can get a recycle bin and put the recycling stuff in the recycle bin.' Now her parents know *exactly* what they need to do to recycle!"

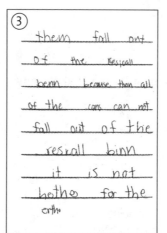
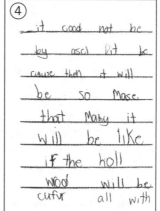

FIG. 15–1   Alyssa's recycling letter

"So I just want to remind you that persuasive writers make sure to include suggestions and warnings to help their readers know how to fix their problems. You can reread your writing and think, 'What extra information can I add to help my reader?' to find places to add a suggestion to give the reader some extra help or a warning to keep the reader safe. You might add these tips to a speech bubble in your picture. Then you can add it to your sentences. You can add warnings and suggestions to all kinds of writing, too: your songs, petitions, letters, and how-to books!"

As Students Continue Working . . .

As children were busy working on a variety of pieces, some returning to petitions and songs while others jumped into the work of procedural texts, I voiced over as kids continued writing. "Writers, remember that when you are writing to make a change, it helps to draw not just any pictures, but pictures that show your reader *exactly* what the problem is and how you hope things will change. You can add zoomed-in drawings and labels or speech bubbles to show this to your readers."

use as a guinea pig, and ask that student to read his or her writing to the others. If the writer read, "Don't throw your garbage on the street!" you could show the class that asking a 'What if . . .' question would result in you asking, "What if everyone left their garbage on the sidewalk?" or "What if the streets were covered with trash?" These 'What if . . .' statements are meant as nudges to help the writer say more. If one partner asks a 'What if . . .' question that counters his partner's proposition, this can rally the writers to argue more forcefully.

You may alternatively notice some of your students struggling with conventions. Again, if several students need help writing more conventionally, this warrants a small group.

You could point to a piece of writing that had hung in a public place but was poorly spelled or hard to read. Maybe you will ask your students to take a stab at reading it as well. Point out that no matter how important the message, if no one can read the sign, no one can do anything to fix the problem. Perhaps then you will then ask your students to read over the writing they have been working on for the last few days. Are there parts that can be made more readable? What can be done to fix their writing so that their message is clear? Have tools on hand for your students to use vowel charts, portable word walls, sentence strips, and so on. Allow them to get started making their writing more readable right there in the meeting area while you go from student to student, providing them with coaching and support.

Adding More Detail by Asking "How?," "Where?," or "What?"

Ask partners to work together to revise their pieces by asking, "How?," "Where?," and "What?" to identify parts that require additional detail.

I called the students to the meeting area, asking them to bring along their writing and revision pens. "Writers, will you meet me on the rug? I have some ideas for ways to help you make your writing even better!" I waited for students to settle on the rug beside their writing partners.

"Thumbs-up if you have again been doing a big variety of writing—perhaps letters and songs, signs and petitions." I scanned the rug quickly surveying responses. "Thumbs-up if you decided to write how-to books to help protect our Earth." Again, I scanned the rug to assess who had decided to take on this new work.

"Wonderful! Well, right now, I've got some new ideas that I want to share with you." I leaned in, as if to relay monumental news. "No matter what kind of persuasive writing you are doing, you can add even more detail to your writing, especially in parts that are not so clear. You can ask, 'How?', 'Where?' and 'What?' to find out more information.

"So right now, Partner 1, will you read your writing out loud to your partner? Partner 2, your job is to stop and ask, 'How?', 'Where?,' and 'What?' to find out more information. Then, Partner 1, you can add those details into your writing! Get started!"

I moved in to coach partners, nudging students to interrupt with questions in parts that called for further elaboration. Then, I prompted students to add these details into their writing.

Editing for Punctuation

Partner Work

Dear Teachers,

You are in the final bend of an ambitious unit for kindergarten writers, and the finish line is fast approaching. In preparation for the celebration that lies ahead, you'll want to remind writers to consider audience, reading and writing their pieces in ways that reflect their feelings and including punctuation marks to communicate these intentions to their readers. Across this session, you'll ask writing partnerships to work together in ways that help young writers begin to understand how oral rehearsal supports the ongoing work of revision and editing.

Remember, as with all of our previous letters, we will not include a complete transcript of the teaching for today, but will instead provide you with a road map to design your own minilesson, mid-workshop teaching point, and teaching share. In this letter, we will help you imagine the teaching you might do today while reminding you, "You are the author of your own teaching." After all, you are the sole source for the needs of your children, assessing and responding to the range of writers in your classroom.

The Common Core Language Standards expect kindergartners to recognize and name end punctuation (CCSS L.K.2). Most of your writers will be well on the way to meeting this expectation. Today you'll teach children to work with partners to reflect on the end punctuation they have already inserted and to consider marks they have yet to include. Together, partners will read their pieces aloud and use punctuation marks as road signs, cueing them to take a stop, use an asking voice, or make it loud. Certainly, this work is much more successful when you teach writers to include punctuation *as they write*, rather than as an afterthought. So, while this session asks students to return to written pieces, today's work also prompts writers to carry this learning forward as they compose new sentences within new pieces.

Of course, this partnership work also answers to the speaking and listening standards, which not only ask kindergartners to participate in collaborative conversations, but also expect kindergartners to speak audibly and express thoughts, feelings, and ideas clearly

Common Core State Standards: W.K.1, W.K.5, RFS.K.1, RFS.K.3, RFS.1.3, SL.K.1, SL.K.2, SL.K.3, SL.K.6, L.K.1, L.K.2, L.K.6

(CCSS SL.K.6)—a standard that you'll continue to help students progress toward as you prepare for the final celebration.

MINILESSON

Your connection will remind your children that writers are also readers, reading and rereading their pieces to fix up their work along the way. You may decide to begin your minilesson by reminding your students of all they have already learned about paying attention to punctuation as they read and using these special marks when they write. Or you may decide to begin by reading a familiar text aloud, perhaps a page from a cherished big book or a charted poem, making sure to read it in a way that ignores any punctuation. Surely, kids will be quick to recognize that you are reading it all wrong, correcting you and giving you reminders to slow down, stop, or change your voice. This sets you up for today's teaching point, instructing your children to be just as mindful of punctuation as they write.

Take some time to compose a teaching point that is concise and clear and that follows the format of the others in this book. There is an art to writing teaching points! One of the things to be aware of is the tendency to phrase teaching points in a way that makes them assignments for the day, rather than strategies that writers can draw upon continuously across their writerly life. Instead of saying, "Today I want to teach you to go back and reread what you wrote yesterday and fix up the punctuation marks," you will want to phrase your teaching point as a lesson that is meant to last a lifetime. You might say, "Today I want to teach you that writers make sure that punctuation marks are in all the right places so that their writing sounds exactly the way they want it to. You can reread your pieces and include the marks that will tell the reader *exactly* how to read it."

Now you'll be ready to model this work with your own teacher demonstration piece or a shared class piece. Perhaps you'll enlarge a page of this piece on chart paper, so that students can easily recognize parts that are punctuated correctly and parts that need marks to tell readers how it should sound. To teach this you might want to share, or fabricate, a page of writing that houses all the mistakes you find in many of your children's pieces, and as you come across these hiccups in your rereading, you'll show kids your process for making those parts much more clear, editing for missing or incorrect punctuation.

During the active engagement, you'll want to give writers an opportunity to practice this process. There are several options for facilitating this practice. You might choose to ask the class to help you with the piece with which you have just modeled, reading a bit further into the piece; or you might move onto a different piece or to the children's. You might also set up partnerships to begin this work on the rug, turning back to a recent piece of their own writing to replicate this work with a peer, rereading pieces aloud to stop one another in places that need a special mark while you coach with lean prompts. "Make it exciting!" "Take a stop." "Huh? Ask it." As children work with partners, you'll want to assess their understanding. These quick assessments will help inform the conferences and small groups you pull, targeting the range of needs you see as you listen in to students.

Of course, when it comes to the link of your minilesson, be watchful of the tendency, again, to make this send-off an assignment. You'll want to restate the teaching point in a way that reminds students to use this strategy whenever they are writing, not just today. If you choose to make this be work that partnerships will do together, you may send partners off together, continuing the work they've begun on the rug. You might also hold a small group on the rug, meeting with students you noticed struggled with this work during the minilesson and providing additional reinforcement and guided practice.

CONFERRING AND SMALL-GROUP WORK

Certainly, you'll have writers who have already begun to explore and use punctuation as they write, while others may ignore these conventions entirely. You'll want to address students within their zone of proximal development, rather than pushing students to adopt a practice that is well above the skill work they're ready for. Decide to use this conferring time to meet with students individually, or in small groups, to support children who may need much more remedial practice with these conventions, or to address students who are growing more and more aware of punctuation yet confusing its proper usage. For example, you may notice some students plop down a period at the end of each line, assuming that the sentence ends when they reach the margin. Others may seem to use marks at random, inserting periods mid-sentence to break apart words. You are also likely to find writers who start off strong, including proper punctuation at the start of their writing, but seemingly fizzle out as they continue on across their piece. Students like these are definitely ready for instruction that guides them to listen for changes in their voice as they read (or plan their sentences) aloud to cue them to correctly add a period, an exclamation point, or a question mark as they write.

You may be worried about your more novice writers, who may still be recording words without leaving finger spaces or be using capital and lowercase letters interchangeably. You might decide to lead a quick interactive writing lesson in a small group with these writers, helping them to use proper capitalization, spacing, and end punctuation to record a short sentence you compose together. Then you can coach children as they transfer these skills to their independent writing.

Perhaps you'll also find time to target some of your more experienced writers, teaching them to use favorite authors as mentors. You may help them study familiar texts to discover ways this author uses punctuation while encouraging them to find places in their own writing to try these same craft moves, perhaps exploring more advanced techniques for manipulating voice across a piece of writing, such as using ellipses to slow the reader down and build tension, or making words big or bold to bring attention to important words within the piece.

MID-WORKSHOP TEACHING

To set up your mid-workshop teaching, you might meet with a child to confer in a way that will address not only individual needs, but will also lend itself to a broader application. For example, you might meet with a partnership and suggest that they can read their pieces to each other and stop at moments when their voices pause, rise to ask a question, or get louder. Then they can remind each other to check to see if the right kind of mark ends that sentence.

Then for your mid-workshop teaching point, you could stop the entire class to share the smart ideas these youngsters came up with, giving the pair total credit while giving your idea social power and reinforcing ongoing practice.

You might also use mid-workshop voiceovers to remind partners to move quickly from reading aloud to the work of revision and editing, quickly fixing up parts to reflect the intended intonation.

SHARE

For your share, you might once again ask children to come back to the meeting area and sit beside their writing partner, now with revised pieces in hand. You may choose to follow up the work that partners began together by asking children to go back once more to read their writing aloud, attending to the newly added punctuation to show how these marks will help others read it properly. Perhaps you'll project a piece of student writing, highlighting the punctuation across the page and demonstrating how it would sound without such cues and how it *now* reads with these important marks.

Have fun!

Lucy & Liz

Speaking Up and Taking a Stand

Planning and Rehearsing Speeches

TODAY'S SESSION PREPARES CHILDREN for the upcoming unit celebration, giving writers an opportunity to look across the pieces they have collected in their folders, marking key parts to share and talk about in the speeches they'll soon deliver. You'll teach students that when presenting these persuasive projects, it helps to make a plan for the words and ideas they'll share with their audience.

You may choose to prepare Post-it notes, or adhesive labels, each marked with prompts such as "One time . . . ," "You should know . . . ," "This is important because . . . ," or "I think . . . " to help your children prepare their speeches during the presentations they'll give. Speeches? Presentations? You might be questioning the possibility of making this a reality in your kindergarten classroom. Envision your young writers standing up in front of a poster board, long pointer in hand, smacking magazine cutouts, photographs, signs, and pieces of their writing flagged with reminders of the stories, ideas, and extra information they want to tell people as they ad lib speeches about their topic.

Today you'll give your students an opportunity to prepare how these speeches might go, planning the sentences they'll want to read and the ideas they'll want to add on when speaking out loud to an audience. You'll also want to provide opportunities for children to read their writing aloud. After all, speeches are a medium intended for ears, and you'll want your students to listen to the way their words sound out loud. To support this endeavor, you'll ask students to work with partners to share their speeches with each other, prompting them to share ideas for ways to make their presentations better—clearer, louder, and more expressive.

The conferring and small-group work you do today will offer additional support, coaching writers and writing partnerships to reread their pieces and make plans for their speeches and presentations. Today you will help children rehearse out loud, perhaps by providing a model to echo or whispering in lean prompts to support the asides kids will make as they elaborate orally on their topics. For example, you'll urge kids to say more, voicing over, "One time . . . " or "Another thing you should know is . . . " or "I think . . . " and so on.

IN THIS SESSION, you'll teach students that writers make a plan for the ideas they want to share when giving a persuasive speech.

GETTING READY

- ✔ Post-it notes labeled with speech prompts (see Teaching and Active Engagement)

- ✔ Littering petition (or other shared writing sample) written during Session 12 small-group work (see Teaching and Active Engagement)

- ✔ A page of speech-prompt-labeled Post-it notes, one for each student (see Link)

- ✔ Student writing folders to select three pieces to publish (see Mid-Workshop Teaching)

- ✔ Paper clips and star-shaped Post-it notes (see Mid-Workshop Teaching)

- ✔ Video clip (http://www.youtube.com/watch?v=ealvk1cSyG8) of a mentor speechmaker (see Share)

- ✔ Chart paper and markers to list strategies for speechmaking (see Share)

COMMON CORE STATE STANDARDS: W.K.1, W.K.5, W.1.1, RFS.K.1, RFS.K.2, RFS.K.3, SL.K.1, SL.K.3, SL.K.6, L.K.1, L.K.2, L.K.6

For today's mid-workshop teaching you will be asking students to read through all of the writing they have accumulated in this bend, choosing their three best to prepare for publication. You can scaffold this process for them by first having

---

"Today you'll give your students an opportunity to prepare how their speeches might go, planning the sentences they'll want to read and the ideas they'll want to add on when speaking out loud to an audience."

them sort their writing into piles: those they have no interest in publishing and those they do. They can then narrow down their favorites to their top three. You may even decide to push them for variety, perhaps choosing at least two different forms of persuasive writing. Either way, be sure to leave them ample time to read over their writing and then make calculated decisions. After all, sending one's writing out into the world is not something to be taken lightly!

And finally, just as you led your children in an inquiry of Lily's letter, studying her writing to discover replicable persuasive strategies, during today's share session, you'll again ask your students to join you in an inquiry of a mentor. You'll notice that the mentor text discussed refers to a short video clip of young boy proudly urging his audience to believe in themselves and to never give up, upon his triumph over training wheels (http://www.youtube.com/watch?v=eaIvk1cSyG8). After all, the work your kindergartners are taking on is that of a speechmaker, and to do this well, it will help to study the work of other young speechmakers. You'll want children to share their observations as they look and listen closely to the young boy, studying his gestures and body language, while listening to his expressive tone. Together, you'll draft a list of what the boy does to captivate his listeners, using this outline of strategies to help kindergartners give equally captivating speeches.

Speaking Up and Taking a Stand
Planning and Rehearsing Speeches

CONNECTION

Tell the students that not only can they write about the things they care about, like the Lorax, but they can speak up as well.

"Each one of you, like the Lorax, cares and uses all kinds of writing to get others to care, too. The Lorax spoke up for what he cared about, saying, 'I speak for the trees!' *You*, also, have to speak up for the people and the places and the problems that need your help. If you stand very tall, speaking loud and clear, maybe your words will reach *lots* of ears. Maybe you can convince a whole crowd of people to care about the things you really care about."

I paused, tapping my chin in thought. "But you know, if you're going to convince a whole crowd of people to help you, you'll need to make plans for the important things you want to make sure to say. Then, speak in ways that *really* get people to listen up!"

❖ **Name the teaching point.**

"Today I want to teach you that presenters make a plan for the words and ideas they want to share with their audience. You can reread your writing and think, 'What sentences are most important? What else do I think? What stories can I tell to say even more?' Then you can mark parts in your writing where you can say more—things you haven't yet written—and rehearse your speech out loud, practicing reading part of it and then saying more."

TEACHING AND ACTIVE ENGAGEMENT

Show students how to use Post-it notes labeled with speech prompts to mark places in their writing where they have a story to tell or other ideas to share.

As I reread my writing, I am going to mark parts that remind me of a story I want to tell or information that I can add on. I know when I give my speech, I'll read part and then I'll just say more.'"

◆ COACHING

Mention of the Lorax is weaved across the unit as a way to rally young writers around the larger cause. Whatever your rally cry, you'll want to keep the energy and enthusiasm up along the way in an effort to keep volume high and especially the joy!

We've found that sometimes teachers worry that persuasive speeches will be scary for children. Push past those worries.

"Let's go back to the petition some of you helped write about the problem with littering. If we were turning it into a speech, we need to find places in it where we could say more. So let's reread it and think." I projected the petition for the students to see as I read.

> Littering is a big problem. We see it in school, on the street, and at the park.

Before continuing, I stopped and turned back to the class. "You know, this part reminds me of a story I could tell to the listeners." I picked up a Post-it note labeled "One time . . ." and placed that Post-it beside the second sentence, adding a talk prompt into the written text. Then I pointed to the Post-it and shared an anecdote. "One time, I was at the park and a little boy threw his popsicle stick right in the bushes! He could have put it in the garbage can, but he finished the last bite and just threw it. So, I had to pick it up!"

Give students an opportunity to find parts in the petition that remind them of stories they want to tell or additional information that is important to share.

I leaned in to address the class. "I could tell that story when I give a speech about this. Do you think if people hear this story, they'll realize that littering is a big problem?" They nodded in total agreement. "Let's keep reading. Show me a thumb if I come to another place where you have ideas for a story you want to tell or information you could explain. I read on.

> We don't like when people throw garbage on the ground because it makes the Earth dirty. Litter hurts plants and flowers. Litter can hurt animals, too.

I looked up from the piece and acknowledged the raised thumbs, signaling students' ideas. "Tell your partner where, exactly, you'd add on. Would your add-on start, 'One time…' like mine? Or maybe your addition would start, "This is important because….' Tell your partner where you'd say more, if you were turning this into a speech, and what you'd say."

"I think that when it says litter hurts the flowers, I could explain that flowers won't grow because of all the garbage," Zaara announced.

"One time, I saw juice boxes and potato chip bags by the trees, and it was yucky," Serena tagged on.

I moved in to listen to others.

"I think that part about that litter hurts animals," Jacob began. "That is important because if there is litter on the street then animals can eat it and choke. Or maybe they can get sick."

Model giving a speech by alternating between reading the petition and telling anecdotes to accompany it.

I quickly marked up the petition with corresponding sticky notes to reflect several of the ideas partners had shared. Then I reconvened the class to demonstrate how these fragments of writing and ideas might sound when delivering a speech out loud. Standing up tall with a pointer in hand, I began.

"Ahem. I want to talk to you about a problem with littering." I tapped my pointer on the first sticky note. 'Littering is a big problem. We see it in school, on the street, and at the park.' One time, I was at a park and a little boy threw his Popsicle stick right into the bushes. He could have put it into the garbage can, but he finished the last bite and just threw it. So I had to pick it up.

"'We don't like when people throw garbage on the ground because it makes the earth dirty.' One time Serena saw juice boxes and potato chip bags by the trees and it was yucky." Pointing at the next sticky note, I added "'Litter hurts plants and flowers. Litter can hurt animals, too. And this is important because animals can eat litter and choke or get sick.'" Again I pointed and read, "'People should recycle!'"

Then I concluded, "Please help us stop littering. Thank you."

After taking a curtsy and sitting back in my chair, I turned to the children. "Class, you each have so many ideas to add about this problem. When you give speeches, you'll want to share the ideas and stories and information that will be most important for people to hear about the topics you have been writing about."

LINK

Send students off with labeled Post-its so that they can begin planning their speeches.

"So remember, if you want to give speeches that get people to really listen, it helps to make a plan for the words and ideas you'll share with your audience. As you reread your writing, you can think, 'What sentences are most important? What else do I think? What stories can I tell to say even more?' Then you can mark those parts and rehearse out loud to practice how your speech might go.

"Each of you will receive a page of labeled sticky notes, just like the ones I used, that you can use to mark up the different parts from all of your best pieces as you plan your speeches and get your projects ready. Remember, speeches are meant to be heard! You'll probably choose to practice the words you want to say out loud so that you can listen to how your speech will go. Just like I did, you can go back and forth between reading parts from your writing and then adding on extra ideas and information.

"Remember, in a few days we are going to be publishing our persuasive writing, getting our ideas out into the world. And we're not just going to read our writing, but we are going to give speeches too, to speak out loud and proud. So the speech planning that you begin today is going to be very important for our writing celebration in a few days."

It's important to make the teaching you do transparent, modeling and naming your process in a way that makes it replicable. You'll want to emphasize the way you move between reading lines of the petition to pointing to the speech prompts to elaborating aloud.

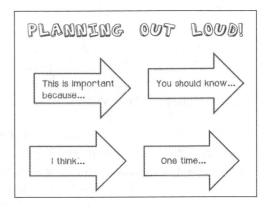

FIG. 17–1

Small-Group Work to Support Student Speechmakers

THROUGHOUT THE YEAR your students have likely become accustomed to reading their writing in front of the class. It is also likely that they are quite comfortable sharing their thinking and stories in front of a large group as well. But combining the two is an entirely new ball game. When do I read? When do I speak? Where do I look? These are all things that your students may be struggling with after today's minilesson.

For today's conferring, instead of working with individual students, you may want to work with partnerships, or even several groups of partnerships together. It will be important that your students practice their speeches with an audience—and for today, an audience whose job it will be to not just listen but provide them with constructive feedback as well. It may be helpful to teach students how to listen and observe—what to be watching for. Perhaps you will provide the listeners with a list of criteria—what they should be on the lookout for. Does the speechmaker look at the audience? Does the speechmaker go back and forth between reading from their writing and telling stories? Does the speechmaker speak out loud and proud, projecting the passion that they feel about their cause through their words and voice?

Other students may be struggling just to come up with the stories that they need to tell for their speeches. It may be helpful to identify these students and then pull them into a small group. Similar to the way you worked off of a shared piece of writing to plan a speech during today's minilesson, you can use writing from one of the students in the group as a writing sample. Walk through the speech-planning process again, using the labeled Post-it notes. Coach the student to read her writing, stopping and marking places where she is reminded of a story she wants to tell or information she thinks is important to share with her audience. It may be that just seeing the process modeled again is enough to get these students going. If that is the case, they can get started, and you can check in with them throughout the remainder of the work period to assess their progress and provide additional assistance. For those students who still need more support, perhaps you will need to coach them through the process in a one-on-one conference.

MID-WORKSHOP TEACHING
Sorting and Selecting Pieces for Publication

I called students over with their writing folders, filled with pieces they had been working on throughout the third bend. Once the class had gathered in the meeting area, I began. "Writers: In just a few short days, we will be having our writing celebration. This celebration is so important, not just because you will finally be sharing your persuasive writing with the world, but for another reason was well. All along, throughout this unit, we have been talking about how persuasive writers write to make things better. They are careful observers of the world, noticing problems and things that need to be made better. And then, writers use their words, just like magic wands, to convince other people to help out and make things better. Over the past few weeks, we've all been writing about ways to make the Earth a cleaner and greener place. Because this idea is so important, and you've done so much writing about it, for this celebration, everyone is going to have the opportunity to publish up to three pieces of writing!" Several students cheered, clearly enthralled with the idea of not being limited to just one piece.

"I asked all of you to bring your writing folders with you to the meeting area, because right now, I'd like you to make some decisions about which pieces you want to publish. As you read through the writing that is in your folder, sort it into two different piles. One pile will be for pieces you may want to publish, and the other pile is for pieces that you do not want to publish. Be sure to think about which pieces show off your best work—the pieces that are the most convincing! Okay? Let's get sorting!"

I moved throughout the hubbub, providing support to students who needed a bit more guidance. By now, choosing pieces to publish was old hat to many of the students.

After students finished sorting their writing into two stacks, I called for their attention. "Excellent sorting, writers. I see some towering stacks of writing as I look around. So exciting! Right now, can everyone please take the pile of writing that you don't want to publish and put it right back into your folder, so it's out of the way?" I paused, giving students an opportunity to put their writing away and then continued. "Okay, now here comes the really hard part, choosing the three pieces that you *do* want to publish. You have worked so hard on all of your writing that I know this will be a difficult decision. But remember, writers have to make choices. Pick pieces that contain ideas you want to make sure get out into the world."

As children worked, I voiced over, "You've written letters, petitions, signs, songs, poems, how-to books. Choose a mix. Once you have your three pieces selected, I'll paper-clip them together, and you can stick a star sticky note right on top of the pile. Tomorrow you'll need to fix and fancy up these pieces. You will only need to plan a speech for *one* of the pieces you pick, though. The other two will be a part of your big poster. Sound like a plan?" Once students had selected and paper-clipped their pieces, I sent them off to continue planning their speeches.

Learning from a Mentor Speechmaker

Let students know that just as they studied mentor texts for writing ideas, they can study speechmakers to learn how to make their speeches better.

I called students over to the meeting area with their three paper-clipped pieces, carefully selected for publication. Once the class had gathered in the meeting area, I began. "Writers, you already know that authors often study the work of other authors to discover ways to make their work smarter, stronger, and more unforgettable. When you look closely at the writing others have made, it can give you ideas for what you might try in your own writing! But guess what? You can do this same kind of work to help you present your speeches. And we're going to do that today!"

I turned to the Smart Board to start up a short video clip of a young boy, proudly sharing his triumph about learning to ride a bike. "Let's look and listen closely to this video of a young boy who finally learned how to ride a bike. When you watch it, I want you to think about what parts stand out to you or give you strong feelings." I played the video from the beginning as the students pinpointed memorable parts. "Show me a thumb if you have a part that really stands out in your mind, one that you remember most from his speech." Thumbs shot up around the room.

"Okay, I am going to give you one more chance to watch the video. This time, as you are watching, think '*How* did he do it? How did he make those parts stand out? What does he do to give his words a lot of power so people will really listen?' Try to answer that big question as you watch it one last time." I played the clip once more as students took careful note of his words, gestures, and expression. Then I prompted the students to turn and talk, sharing the parts they remembered most and thinking together about how the young boy made those parts so memorable. While partners talked, I listened in.

Then I brought the group back together. "Let's make a list of ways you noticed the boy made his speech so convincing."

"He talked really loud. Like he was yelling, but not really," Anna piped up.

"Yeah, and he got up on the thing to be taller so he could talk up high," Serena added.

"I can tell he was really happy because he was talking like he was really proud of himself," Gabriella joined in.

"Oh! He gave a thumbs up," Shane laughed.

"And peace signs, like this, see," Diego demonstrated, giggling.

I continued to collect these ideas, while drafting a class list.

"Wow! What smart ideas! Tomorrow, when you are fixing and fancying up your writing, you will have another opportunity to practice your speeches. Maybe you'll want to try out some of these things from the chart so you can speak just as passionately as this little boy did and speak in a way that makes people really listen!"

Fixing and Fancying Up for Publication Using the Super Checklist

IN THIS SESSION, you'll teach students that writers revise and edit their writing before publication using writing tools, in this case a checklist.

GETTING READY

✔ Student-selected pieces for publication, paper-clipped together (see Connection)

✔ "Make People Really Listen!" chart from previous session (see Connection)

✔ Double-sided pages for students (Super Checklist), one side with the Opinion Writing Checklist and the other side with the Editing Checklist, three copies (see Link) 🖈

✔ Enlarged copy of the Opinion Writing Checklist, Grades K and 1 (see Teaching) 🖈

✔ Enlarged copy of the Editing Checklist (see Teaching) 🖈

✔ Littering petition, or other shared writing sample, rewritten to contain several obvious errors that you want to edit for (see Teaching and Active Engagement)

✔ Mailing labels or other white stickers to use for editing (see Teaching and Active Engagement)

✔ Poster boards for each student (see Mid-Workshop Teaching)

✔ Petition sign-in sheets for each student (see Mid-Workshop Teaching)

✔ Binder clips and glue sticks (see Mid-Workshop Teaching)

COMMON CORE STATE STANDARDS: W.K.1, W.K.5, W.1.1, RFS.K.1, RFS.K.2, RFS.K.3, SL.K.1, SL.K.5, L.K.1, L.K.2

T ODAY YOU'LL SET OUT TO HELP YOUR CHILDREN take one last inventory of their writing—making final revisions and edits to prepare for publication and tomorrow's celebration! Across this unit, you've guided students to work with the aid of a checklist, reflecting on their pieces to make plans for revision. At the start of today's session, you'll provide students with this same Opinion Writing Checklist, but also with a familiar editing checklist, thus presenting a Super Checklist—challenging your young writers to use all they have learned about opinion writing across this unit, along with all they have learned about spelling and conventions this year in kindergarten.

Just as your students are equipped with a checklist, you'll want to keep your rubric by your side as you meet with writers during today's conferences and small groups. The Opinion Writing Learning Progression will support your own inventory as you take into account the work your children are *now* doing. You'll want to use this teacher-facing rubric to determine what final supports you'll need to provide before the end of this unit. You may choose to spend this last day working with small groups of writers who have similar needs, coaching them to use a particular strategy with stronger understanding.

During this session, you'll give children an opportunity to not only *fix*, but also to *fancy*. You'll ask your students to prepare poster boards, on which they'll present their three published pieces. You may decide to have your own poster already prepared to give students an example of the language, placement, and size of the titles they'll write.

For today's share session, you'll organize a museum walk, allowing your children to tour the classroom and read their classmates' final projects. Think of this as a private *wrap party*, giving a chance for your "cast of writers" to celebrate the very impressive work they've accomplished this month, before it's shared with the public. After all, you've directed a commendable unit of study, and it's important to honor the pursuits you and your kindergartners have made—perhaps even sparking a lasting drive to venture on with this initiative, walking away from this unit not just as stronger writers, but as writers who use words to seek change and strive to make things better.

Fixing and Fancying Up for Publication Using the Super Checklist

CONNECTION

Refer to the "Make People Really Listen!" chart. Let students know they will have a chance to practice their speeches again today.

Students gathered on the rug, paper-clipped pieces in hand. "Writers, I am super excited for our workshop today. This is it! It is almost time for us to send our writing out into the world and share our ideas with others. You have been working so hard, writing to make a difference. And now, speaking to make a difference, too! You'll have some time today to continue to practice your speeches. Don't forget to do all those things that little boy in the video did to make people really listen." I gestured toward the "Make People Really Listen!" chart we had made the previous session. "In addition to practicing our speeches, we have a few other things we need to do before we can celebrate all of our fantastic writing."

Name the teaching point.

"Today I want to teach you that writers need to make sure that their writing says exactly what they want it to say and also make sure that it is readable, before they send it out into the world."

TEACHING AND ACTIVE ENGAGEMENT

Introduce the Super Checklist to the students as a tool to use to get their writing ready for publication.

"We have talked so many times before about how writers use tools to help them with their writing. Today I have two very important tools for you to use. Neither of them will be new to you. In fact, you've used them so many times before, you could probably teach *me* how to use them instead of me teaching *you*." Giggles erupted through the classroom as children thought about the role reversal.

"I've put these tools together on one sheet of paper for you, to make one handy dandy Super Checklist for you to use to get your persuasive writing fixed and fancied up before publishing." I held up a copy of the double-sided page for all to see. "On one side of the page is the Opinion Writing Checklist. We used this *way* back, a few weeks ago, when we were writing about problems that we were seeing in our classroom and school. Do you remember shooting for the stars?" Kids nodded in agreement, and I gestured toward the enlarged copy of the Opinion Writing Checklist on

Using language that reminds students of what they already know, rather than using additional time to reteach or explain, places more responsibility on children.

display in the writing center. "You can go over all of the items on the Opinion Writing Checklist to make sure that your writing is as strong as it can be. If you realize that you have forgotten to do something on this list, now is your chance to fix it! Now, the *other* side of this paper has *another* writing tool on it—an editing checklist. After you finish revising your writing using the Opinion Writing Checklist, you'll need to switch gears and become an editor! Writer editor!" I flipped the paper over, showing the editing checklist. "We've used this editing checklist before, when we were getting our true stories and our how-to books ready to publish. I've added some new items to the checklist, though, since you have grown so much as writers since the last time we used it. When you put on your editor hat," I pulled a pretend cap onto my head, "these are the things you'll need to be looking for." I pointed to the enlarged copy of the editing checklist that was displayed on the easel and read each item. The Opinion Writing Checklist, Grades K and 1 and the Editing Checklist can be found on the CD-ROM.

Revise your writing in front of the class using the Opinion Writing Checklist side of the Super Checklist. Give students an opportunity to try this as well.

Opinion Writing Checklist

	Kindergarten	NOT YET	STARTING TO	YES!	Grade 1	NOT YET	STARTING TO	YES!
	Structure				**Structure**			
Overall	I told, drew, and wrote my opinion or likes and dislikes about a topic or book.	☐	☐	☐	I wrote my opinion or my likes and dislikes and said why.	☐	☐	☐
Lead	I wrote my opinion in the beginning.	☐	☐	☐	I wrote a beginning in which I got readers' attention. I named the topic or text I was writing about and gave my opinion.	☐	☐	☐
Transitions	I wrote my idea and then said more. I used words such as *because*.	☐	☐	☐	I said more about my opinion and used words such as *and* and *because*.	☐	☐	☐
Ending	I had a last part or page.	☐	☐	☐	I wrote an ending for my piece.	☐	☐	☐
Organization	I told my opinion in one place and in another place I said why.	☐	☐	☐	I wrote a part where I got readers' attention and a part where I said more.	☐	☐	☐
	Development				**Development**			
Elaboration	I put everything I thought about the topic (or book) on the page.	☐	☐	☐	I wrote at least one reason for my opinion.	☐	☐	☐
Craft	I had details in pictures and words.	☐	☐	☐	I used labels and words to give details.	☐	☐	☐
	Language Conventions				**Language Conventions**			
Spelling	I could read my writing.	☐	☐	☐	I used all I knew about words and chunks of words (*at, op, it*, etc.) to help me spell.	☐	☐	☐
	I wrote a letter for the sounds I heard.	☐	☐	☐	I spelled all the word wall words right and used the word wall to help me spell other words.	☐	☐	☐
	I used the word wall to help me spell.	☐	☐	☐				

"I thought we could start by using our Super Checklist to edit a piece of the writing that we've done together. Let's reread our littering petition and then start with the Opinion Writing Checklist side of our Super Checklist." I projected the littering petition and read it aloud.

> Littering is a big problem. we see it in scool, on the street, and at the park We Don't like when people throw garbage on the ground. we don't like when people throw garbage on the ground becuz it makes the Earth dirty Litter hurts plants and flowers. Litter Can hurt animals, too.

I began to think out loud, ticking through each item on the Opinion Writing Checklist. "Let's see here, 'I wrote my opinion in the beginning.' Oh yes, I definitely did that. Littering is a problem. That is my opinion. Okay, next, 'I had details in pictures and words.' Yes, right here," I pointed to the second sentence in the petition, "we wrote about all the places we see litter. Those are details telling why littering is bad, because we see garbage in school, on the street, and in the park." I continued ticking off bullets from the checklist, thinking out loud as I self-assessed the writing sample. Finally, I came to one that was not evident in my writing. "Hmm, 'I put everything I thought about the topic (or book) on the page.' I wonder if I could say more, maybe add something about the way littering makes me feel. Maybe that will help my reader know that I really care about this. What do you all think? Go ahead right now and turn and talk. What could I add to my writing to show my reader that I really care?" Students turned and talked while I listened in. After a few minutes I called the group back together.

"So, writers, how do I revise my writing? What can I add to it?" I asked the group.

"I think that you could write about your feelings," suggested Will. "If you tell about your feelings, how littering makes you feel, your readers will know how much you care. Like, does littering make you feel mad? You could write, 'I get so mad when I see garbage on the street!'"

"I have another idea!" shouted Alyssa. "I bet people would know you really care if you tell about something that you do to fix it! Sometimes when I see litter at the park I just pick it up and throw it in a trash can. Maybe other people will want to help, too!"

"Thanks, friends, these are some great suggestions!" I replied. I grabbed a revision strip and began to write. "Both great ideas. Alyssa, I do the same thing! When I see garbage in the hallways right here in school I always pick it up and throw it out. I am going to add that to my writing!" I grabbed a revision strip, wrote the sentence, and attached it to the petition.

Edit your writing in front of the class using the Editing Checklist side of the Super Checklist. Give students an opportunity to edit the writing sample using the checklist.

"Okay, writers, let's try switching caps. Editors, ready? Put on those editing caps!" I mimed putting a cap on my head, and the kids did the same. "Let's look again at the littering petition, this time as editors. We can do one thing at a time, right down through each bullet on the Editing Checklist. So let's start with the first thing on the checklist, 'Capital letters at the beginning of a sentence and the rest lowercase.' I am going to read through each sentence in my petition. If I come to a capital letter or a lowercase letter where they don't belong, I can just use one of these stickers to cover up the mistake and rewrite the letter!" I began to read, pointing under each word with my finger. When I got to the second sentence, I stopped. "Would you look at that!" I exclaimed. "I started that sentence with a lowercase letter. That *w* should be a capital, since it is at the beginning of the sentence. I need to take care of that." I voiced over my actions as I used one of the mailing labels to cover the lowercase *w* and wrote in a capital *W*. I continued reading through the petition, checking for capital and lowercase letters.

"Editors, now it is your turn. The next thing we need to look for is word wall words. Those should *always* be spelled correctly. I am going to start back at the beginning of the petition, and this time we'll be on the lookout for word wall words. If you notice that there is one spelled incorrectly, thumbs up, okay? Let's get started." Again, I began to read, pointing under each word as I did so. The minute I got to the word *school* spelled incorrectly, thumbs shot up all around me. I stopped reading. "Ah, it looks like the editors have found something!"

"School!" declared Serena. "*School* is spelled wrong. Look! It's on the word wall. You need to fix that." Again, I used the mailing label to cover up the misspelling and correctly wrote *school* on top of it, carefully copying from the word wall.

LINK

Send students off with their Super Checklist to begin revising and editing in preparation for publication.

"So, writers, this is it! Today is your last day to work on your writing before our celebration. Each one of you will get three copies of the Super Checklist—one for each piece of writing you will be publishing. This checklist will be a great tool for you to use to make sure that your writing says everything you want it to say and is readable. Everyone ready to get started?"

Small-Group Work to Support Student Editors

A S YOU HELP YOUR STUDENTS PREPARE FOR PUBLICATION, your instinct may be to help them fix every little error you see in their writing, to edit for every misstep. However, keep in mind that today and always, your goal is to help your students do the best work that they can, at this moment in time, and teach them skills and strategies that will last a lifetime. The greater goal is about the process, not the product.

As the year has progressed, your expectations for your students as writers and editors has progressed as well. Your editing checklist, growing over time, now contains a new bullet point. You now expect your students to edit for multiple things: capitalization, word wall words, and ending punctuation.

To help move students along toward publication and support as many of them as you can, it may make sense to create several small groups, based on what you are noticing students' particular needs are. Perhaps you have several students who are still struggling with automaticity around the spelling of word wall words. Maybe you will pull them into a group and work with white boards, to do an interactive writing lesson. Remind them of the steps to follow to turn a word into a snap word. Use words that you are noticing they are still struggling with, word wall words that are misspelled in their persuasive pieces. Then help them read through their pieces, looking for places where they need to edit for these words.

A few sessions ago you taught a lesson on ending punctuation. While some students may have internalized this process, learning to listen for how their voice changes as they read their writing and inserting the proper punctuation accordingly, it is not atypical to still have students who are simply dropping a period or exclamation point at the end of every line or even just one at the end of their entire piece. In this case, you may want to create your own writing sample to work on together. Your piece should house many punctuation mistakes, and you should be sure to read it as such. Students will laugh at your speed and breathlessness, as you read an entire piece, not pausing once to stop and take a breath. Remind them that ending punctuation separates thoughts. Have them work with partners, reading their writing out loud,

MID-WORKSHOP TEACHING
Creating Poster Boards to Display Published Writing

I called for students' attention, briefly interrupting their editing and revision work. "Writers, there is one last thing you need to do to get ready for tomorrow. Everyone will need to make a poster to display their writing. Your poster is like a giant cover for your project! Just like when you made covers for your true stories and your how-to books, you can write a big title at the top to grab people's attention!" Holding up my own poster board, I shared an example. "Maybe you'll make your title a question to get others to wonder, like 'What Can You Do to Help the Earth?' Or maybe you'll use your title to say the most important thing people should do to help you, like 'Help Pick Up Litter! Keep the Earth Clean!'" I held up a second example, spotlighting how the title was written in large letters at the top. "Whatever you decide, it'll be important that your title is big so people can see it at tomorrow's celebration."

"You should also create a sign-in sheet, a petition, to display next to your writing. That way, your guests will have a chance to show they care, too. They can sign their names to agree to help your cause! Make sure to write your name at the top of the sign-in sheet, and you can put the same title that is on your poster across the top of the sign in sheet as well."

As Students Continue Working . . .

"Writers, I am placing binder clips and glue sticks in the middle of every table so you can attach your pieces to your poster board. You'll use the binder clip to clip on the piece that your speech is about and use the glue sticks to paste the other two pieces. This way, you'll be able to show off all your writing!"

stopping only when they have a punctuation mark instructing them to do so. Then they can reread their writing, this time stopping where one thought ends, and inserting the appropriate punctuation.

Celebration Preview
A Museum Walk

Set up a museum walk so that students have the opportunity to read over each other's posters before the celebration.

Before the share, I asked students to spread their posters out around the classroom. "I thought it would be great for us to take some time right now to take a museum walk. Check out each other's posters, before all of the visitors come tomorrow. Sound like a good idea?" After a few minutes of wandering through the classroom, reading over the posters, I called students to the meeting area.

"Tomorrow we'll have many visitors coming to read your writing and listen to your speeches about your topics. Remember, persuasive writers have a job, and that is to rally people to action. You believe and care about your topics, and your job is to make *others* believe and care, too! You've written these fantastic pieces and now prepared fabulous speeches to go with them. But it's also important that once the celebration is over, your writing is still out there, in public, for all to see. After all, you don't just want the visitors who come to the celebration tomorrow to help you fix the problems you wrote about. You want everyone in the world to help you! And what better way to do that than to display your writing, for all the world to see?

"Now that you've created a poster to display your writing, you can find places throughout the school, or maybe even the community, to display your writing. And then maybe other people will want to help out and make a difference, too!"

The Earth Day Fair
An Author's Celebration

ear Teachers,

You've done it! Hurrah! Or we should say, you *and* your students have done it! What may have seemed like a lofty goal at the onset—kindergarteners noticing problems in their school, community, and world and writing to rally others to action—may not feel so impossible anymore. That is because not only have your five- and six-year-olds become experts at living with open eyes to imagine ways the world can be a better place, but you have also worked in magical ways to help scaffold this process. By beginning in the world of your classroom and gradually extending the lens further and further outward, your students were able to better understand larger challenges and issues in the world and to write about these issues in ways that convince others to join the cause. How could anyone *not* join in and help out?

And now here you are, ready to celebrate all of the hard work you and your students have put forth over the last month. Since the purpose of this unit is writing to make a change, we feel it is important that others hear your students' voices, helping their words reach ears outside your classroom community. After all, if you want to call others to action, they'll need to hear what you have to say first! Additionally, your students have been working hard planning and rehearsing speeches, and now they will need an audience to listen! Our suggestion is that you set up an Earth Day Fair of some sort. It need not be especially big or extravagant, or even take place outside of your classroom; although imagine how empowering it would be for your little ones to host their final celebration in the gymnasium or the schoolyard—some public setting where a wider audience would be reached. We suggest you invite people outside your immediate classroom community, perhaps family members or a class of fifth graders or other adults from the school or neighborhood.

PREPARATION

Over the last several days, your students have prepared poster boards to display the three pieces of writing they have chosen to publish. We suggest that you display these posters

COMMON CORE STATE STANDARDS: W.K.6, RFS.K.1, RFS.K.2, RFS.K.3, SL.K.1, SL.K.3, SL.K.6, L.K.6

around the classroom or wherever you host your celebration, with students stationed beside their work, ready to talk about their topics and answer any questions the guests may have. Don't forget to have the student-created petition and sign-in sheets close by. This way, guests will have an opportunity to show they care, signing up to join the fight for this important cause! You may decide to assign students to several small groups ahead of time, perhaps no more than four children per group. When it is time to give the speeches, each child in the group will rotate to the stations of the other group members, listening to the speeches.

THE CELEBRATION
The Earth Day Fair

As guests begin to arrive, invite them to take a stroll through the fair. Once you notice that most of your guests have arrived, you'll probably want to momentarily interrupt, thanking everyone for coming and explaining how the celebration will unfold. Tell your guests that after they have a chance to tour the Earth Day Fair, they will have the opportunity to listen to several speechmakers speak on behalf of their cause. For now, encourage guests to cycle through, reading the various poster boards, signing petitions, as well as asking questions of the writers.

The Speeches

After guests have been given sufficient time to tour the fair, you can break off into the assigned small groups. Be sure to spread the groups throughout the room. If your audience contains family members, simply ask them to join their child. If you have guests from the school as your visitors, quickly ask them to spread across the groups, to keep the numbers fairly even. Group members, students, and visitors alike will rotate together to each group members' station. You may want to explain to the visitors that for this portion of the celebration, your students will not simply be reading their writing aloud, but instead will be delivering speeches. Remind your students to unclip from their poster the writing they will be giving their speech from. Stress to your students the importance of speaking up loud and proud, speaking with tons of feeling, because after all, they feel passionately about their causes! You may decide to use sound recorders or video cameras to film these presentations, perhaps even uploading them to a school blog, helping your students' words reach even more ears!

You have delivered an indelible message to your young writers, helping children truly understand the words of Dr. Seuss, through his faithful Lorax: "Unless someone like you cares a whole awful lot, nothing is going to get better, it's not." But it's evident that you and your kindergartners *do* care a whole awful lot, and the words they've written and spoken with heart will help make a change in so many remarkable ways.

Thank you.

Lucy & Liz

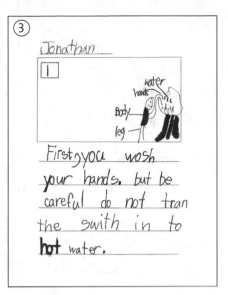

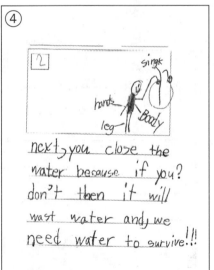

FIG. 19–1   Jonathan's how-to book teaches steps to avoid wasting water, including warnings, suggestions, and important information to persuade readers

First, you wash your hands. But be careful do not turn the switch in to hot water. Next, you close the water because if you don't then it will waste water and, we need water to survive!!! And . . . finally you make sure there are no drips so turn the switch really tight!

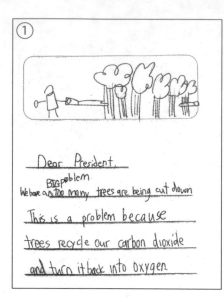

① Dear President,
We have BIG problem too many trees are being cut down This is a problem because trees recycle our carbon dioxide and turn it back into oxygen.

② One time I saw a tree cut down, and that place had no other trees so I couldnt breathe as well as the place (In front of my house) with more

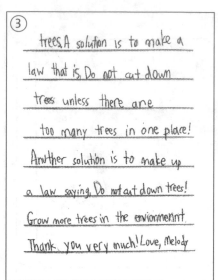

③ trees. A solution is to make a law that is Do not cut down trees unless there are too many trees in one place! Another solution is to make up a law saying, Do not cut down trees! Grow more trees in the enviormenint. Thank you very much! Love, Melody

FIG. 19–2 Melody's letter works to persuade her reader through the use of precise information, comparisons, and several solutions.

Der scooll dont liter or else are scooll will be derty and one day when I was Driving and we wher going slow I sow a

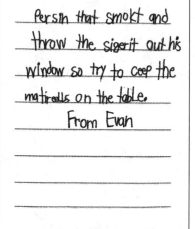

Persin that smokt and throw the sigerit out his window so try to coep the matirells on the table.
From Evan

FIG. 19–3 Evan's letter tells a story about a time he witnessed the problem first hand.

Dear School, Don't litter or else our school will be dirty and one day when I was driving and we were going slow I saw a person that smoked and threw the cigarette out his window so try to keep the materials on the table.

dER sanut Ashn can You cLenThe sreet? PePLLiddR

a LoT. MaKe sor The STreTISCLen LOVE zaara

FIG. 19–4 Zaara's letter addresses an audience that can help with the problem.

Dear Sanitation, Can you clean the street? People litter a lot. Make sure the street is clean. Love, Zaara

GRADE K: PERSUASIVE WRITING OF ALL KINDS

FIG. 19–5   Margaret's how-to book includes pictures and words that help teach a sequence of steps to fix a problem.

First you pick up the trash. Next you find a recycle bin. Third you throw it out.

FIG. 19–6   Sebastian's how-to book includes the steps readers should take to recycle properly.

First you should recycle because it is good for the earth. Next you find a blue bin. Last you put the cans in the recycling bin.